Awaken to the Here and Now

Ending Your Search for Enlightenment

by
Kevin F. Duffy

www.awakentothehereandnow.com

ENDORSEMENTS

ACKNOWLEDGEMENTS

I would like thank Joseph D'Ambrosio and Dennis Jacobi for their considerable efforts in reading and commenting on the first draft. Their insights and encouragement were extremely valuable in the completion of this project.

FOREWORD

Important: Read This Introduction

If you are like me, you probably do not always read introductions. This really is different as it explains some important concepts necessary to make this book more than just an interesting read. This book will change your life if approached correctly.

When I arrived at Purdue University in 1975, I was a devout catholic and I attended Mass every Sunday. My feelings about church doctrines and teachings were conflicted. A lot of it did not seem correct or consistent. I was interested in having a relationship with God and an understanding of my purpose on earth and beyond. Since I grew up catholic and attended a catholic grade school this was the only view I had ever known. To this date, I am grateful for this upbringing, because it was this path from birth to present that brought me to where I am today. It was also responsible for developing my moral compass and the cultural context of who I am.

The first glimmerings of the idea that there were other paths of understanding came to me in my freshman European History class where I learned that for much of Europe's early history the Church and government where pretty much one and the same. Most appalling was that the Church seemed to put its own political interests and survival above all else. This was a real shock to me, because I learned that the Church's only purpose was to help the parishioners develop a personal relationship with God and live a life that would ensure their entrance into heaven. My church was failing to give me the answers for what I was searching. I knew there had to be more than just blind and obedient faith.

During that same time, I discovered that Satsang classes and meditation groups were available around campus that focused on direct personal self-development. I began attending these on a regular basis. I also began to read and study different approaches to the Eastern disciplines as well. I signed up for a credited university course called the Philosophy of Eastern Religions. That turned out to be the most interesting and exciting college course I have ever taken through three college degrees. After that, I was full bore into meditation, self-realization and on the hunt for spiritual enlightenment for the next thirty plus years.

During the last several years, I began meditating one to two times a day with a sense of urgency to attain enlightenment. In the past, I occasionally had mystical experiences during my meditations, but now they started happening regularly and with greater intensity. I was so excited about the experiences. I wanted to share how I had attained this level of awareness, so I began outlining a book. I wanted to teach others what I had learned, so they could get to this level of awareness quickly.

Although I did not feel that I had attained enlightenment at this point, I felt that I was rapidly approaching it. I began to review some of the dozens of books on my bookshelf about enlightenment for background material and I reread some of them with renewed interest. For the most part I recognized all the concepts and they all made sense in context of my new understanding of who and what I was. Nothing was new here. The problem was that they were only registering conceptually as they always had and what I was experiencing was beyond conceptual. I needed to figure it out how to convey this information in a way that others could cross the chasm from conceptual to non-conceptual.

I began to meditate with this question in mind and in a short time, something unexpected happened. I bridged from the conceptual to the non-conceptual. This was a new non-conceptual understanding than that of my recent mystical experiences. I fully non-conceptually realized my non-duality, who, and what I truly am. The mystical experiences were just another distraction. They were not what I was looking for. They were decoys. What I was really looking was quite different and unexpected, non-conceptual enlightenment. That was my first big revelation.

How to teach others to bridge this gap from conceptual to non-conceptual self-realization became my next driving search. I set the thirteen-page outline aside as it held no real value anymore and began to meditate on the second question. The entire outline of this book and workshops came into my awareness. The answer to this question was my second revelation and the genesis of this book.

Here is the thing. Enlightenment is not hard to attain. It is right in front of you. It has been with you your entire life. It is your birthright. You do not have to search for thirty years or meditate for twenty. You do not have to pay homage or worship any guru or master to attain it.

There are a few pre-requisites that you can choose to fulfill or not. If you do not choose to fulfill them, you will not be able to recognize enlightenment.

There are many paths to enlightenment including thirty plus years of meditating, but most are not necessary. The direct path presented here for most, will take a few hours to get the first glimpses and a few months to maintaining lucid wakefullness as a normal state of awareness.

Reading this work sequentially and maintaining an appropriate cadence are important factors to ensure the desired results of reading this book. Reading the book slowly enough so that you have the time to integrate fully the concepts before attempting to cross the threshold is very important. That is, when you read the concepts throughout the book give yourself time to fully absorb and think about the implications of what they mean. One of the many paradoxes of this approach is that you need to understand the concepts well, before you can get to the non-conceptual. Once you are at the non-conceptual, the concepts will be of little use to you except to teach others. You will not need the concepts any longer.

It is more about taking the journey than reading book, because if you only read the book you are not going anywhere. You will be stuck in the conceptual. You need to move to the non-conceptual.

Last and not least, I am not asking you to believe anything I tell you. This is not about belief. It is beyond belief. Belief is a hope or a desire that something will turn out to be true. The truth or the knowing is going to happen to you on this journey. You will no longer need belief, you will non-conceptually know and you will become.

This is an exciting journey and because you are reading these words right now, it is happening to you right now. As you will see later, right now is the only time anything happens anyway. Enjoy the ride.

Chapter 1

ENLIGHTENMENT

Enlightenment is Not Difficult to Realize.

Jesus said, "One who seeks will find. The door will be opened to one who knocks."

Gospel of Saint Thomas (94)

Your search for enlightenment ends right here, right now. This is a bold statement, but if you choose to proceed, you can realize your own enlightenment now. If you have been searching for many years, it may seem counter to everything you have come to believe. You do not have to be born with a destiny to become enlightened. You do not need to sit in a Himalayan cave for twenty years or study with a guru for thirty. It does not take discipline, hard work, hours of meditation, or attainment of mystical experiences or powers. It is neither experiential nor attainable. It is only realizable.

Enlightenment as commonly perceived does not exist outside of the illusion. By the illusion, I mean the everyday organic reality that most people accept as the true reality. The commonly perceived concept of enlightenment exists only within this illusion. True enlightenment exists only in the context of a realization of your true self, the Brahman, the One. The Brahman is the Hindu concept of the unchanging, infinite, divine substrate of all energy, matter, time, space and existence. You cannot attain it, because what you seek, you already are. The difference between those who are enlightened and those who are not, is that the former know it. They do not believe they are enlightened, they non-conceptually recognize their enlightenment. They have ended their search.

Beyond Belief

> Jesus said, "Recognize what is before your face and what is obscure to you will become disclosed unto you. For there is nothing obscure that will not become shown forth."

> Gospel of Saint Thomas (5)

You may be thinking enlightenment is not going to happen for you, and if it does, it is going to be a long hard struggle. You may also think you are not worthy or have not earned the right. Neither of these thoughts is true unless you want them to be. If you have a strong and earnest desire and a willingness to let go of some long held beliefs, you can realize enlightenment right now. You will be able to revalidate your realization repeatedly until it becomes second nature. Once you come to this realization, you will not lose it. Your search will be over.

Enlightenment is not about faith or belief. It is beyond belief. Once you become aware of your own enlightenment, belief or faith will no longer be necessary. You will be beyond belief. Faith and belief rely on hope or trust that something will be true. If you are not absolutely sure or you do not know non-conceptually that something is true, you must take it on faith or belief that it is. If there is some doubt, you must keep telling yourself that you must have faith or belief. To go beyond belief is to come to a non-conceptual understanding of enlightenment. In doing so, enlightenment is beyond belief, experience, and intellectual understanding.

To recognize your enlightenment is for you to recognize your current awareness and to snap out of your daydream. The jargon and language used to describe this process is limited. As limited as it is, it will suffice to get to the realization you are seeking. We will use concepts to catalyze the non-conceptual understanding. This will become clearer as you progress through the material. The language will be contradictory at times, but it will all make sense upon recognition. For instance, you can say that enlightenment is obtainable and enlightenment is not obtainable or that you are everything and you are nothing and they are all correct. Be patient, it will all fall into place.

You will discover the meaning of life, the ultimate truth, universe, and God. Fundamental and irreversible changes will occur to your perception. If you are satisfied with your current beliefs and have no doubts, maybe you should read no further. Proceed only if you want to know the truth at the non-conceptual level and if this is the path, you want to tread.

Within this book, you will see references to the Ego. From purely a psychological point of view, the Ego is one of three identities that are associated with a person's overall self-identity; the other two are the Super Ego and the ID. For the purposes of this book, the ego is referring to the collective self-identity of the Ego, Super Ego and ID.

What you will learn, if you decide to proceed, is all good, not to be feared, and will be celebrated once you are liberated to see yourself as you truly are. In short, when you have completed your self-inquiry as outlined in this book, you will know with confidence that you "get it." You will not be saying that you "get it" to impress yourself (ego) or others. You will "get it!" The purpose of this book is to point you in the right direction, to show you where and how to look in order to see and know your true self. You will be both the teacher and the student. This book is the roadmap that will guide you along the path of self-discovery.

After 30 years of meditating, and studying the teachings from various gurus, teachers, books, CDs, tapes, and lectures, I finally got it. It takes one perspective, one thought, or one perception for it to click. As you will later come to understand, choice has little to do with it in the end anyway. There is no requirement that you need to do anything in excess or make this difficult, unless that is what you do.

I am uncomfortable announcing that I "got it," because it may sound as if I am bragging and telling you that I am somehow different, more advanced, or better than you are. None of these are true. The only difference between someone who is enlightened and those who are not is that the former know it and recognize it. If any guru, author, or teacher tells you that they are more enlightened, better, or chosen- they are not. They are trying to boost their own ego. If they really are enlightened, they would know, in the same way you will soon know, that there are no levels of enlightenment only that you get it or you do not.

The reason I bring up my lengthy struggle at all, is to illustrate 99% of the efforts I made were not on the direct path to self-realization. As you will see later in this book, this circuitous route, in my case, was necessary, because these were the choices I made. You can skip all the unnecessary searching, discipline, practice, meditation and financial expenditures by walking the direct path. What you are reading right in the Here and the Now is the direct path that you can take right now. It is an experience in the chain-of-events of your path of this life. Take the step and see where it leads. Nothing ventured, nothing gained.

Recognizing your enlightenment takes little effort or time. This is also a bold statement but the proof is in the pudding. It does take the courage to let go and give in to the truth you will soon know. Prove it for yourself. I would ask that you suspend your beliefs, until you get to the end of the book. Asking you to believe anything is not necessary. You will know what you need to know. Beliefs for, or against, will be discarded in the end.

If you had never seen the ocean up close and your parents told you that seawater is blue, you would probably believe them. You would take it on faith that seawater is blue because you trust your parents and you always assumed that they were reasonably intelligent. Beliefs typically develop in this way. Someone in apparent authority, a teacher, author, rabbi, priest, or other figure tells you that something is true and unless there is some reason for your not to believe him or her you will take it on faith that it is true.

If later on in life, I told you that seawater was not blue and you may not believe me, because you already believe the opposite from someone you trust to be correct. After all, I am just some nameless, faceless author. We could argue about our differences of opinion or you could conduct your own inquiry and find out for yourself. To conduct this inquiry you could go to the sea and look at the water in your cupped hands. You would come to realize that it was not blue. Your belief about seawater being blue and any argument about it would be unnecessary from that point forward. You discovered that seawater was not blue, because you investigated and saw for yourself. Your new knowingness had nothing to do with me convincing you to accept my beliefs over your parent's beliefs. Your parents did not give you maliciously false information; they just passed their beliefs on to you, as they knew them to be.

I will not give you the new knowledge. I will point a few things out to you. It will be up to you to decide if you want to believe it on faith or to investigate it for yourself. It is also up to you to decide if you are happy with your current beliefs. If you are open to the possibility that some of your beliefs can be proven false, you can investigate it for yourself and come to a new understanding of reality that is beyond belief.

You can find out what is true as in the seawater example above. You will prove this to yourself. My contribution is to point you in a direction that will allow you to investigate the truth within yourself first hand. You can come to your own conclusions and you do not have to believe me or anyone else about your true nature.

Sincerity is Paramount

> You are ripe for enlightenment when you want nothing else. In order to be born you have to spend nine months getting bigger and bigger. For enlightenment, you have to get smaller and smaller until you disappear completely.
>
> Sri Poonja (Papaji)[1]

Sincerity and earnestness are the important determinants in whether you will or will not gain recognition. If you have a burning desire to know the truth about whom and what you are, whether it is from years of searching or suffering, you will get it. If you are ripe and ready to get on with it, ready to let go of misconceptions you have been living with during a lifetime, your search ends now. It may take hours, days, weeks or months at the most. You do not need to take anything on faith, save the occasional short transition period from one concept to the next. In the end, even these short periods of "take my word for it, for a moment," will no longer be necessary. I think you may not be able to get it if you are not willing to suspend or allow for variation in your own beliefs.

Unfortunately, some of the authors, teachers, and gurus either haven't recognized enlightenment, have no intention of helping anyone else, or they cannot present it in a way that makes it attainable for many. I have run across a lot of the above. Ego and financial gain are the drivers for some of these teachers. I have no problem paying teachers for their time and effort, as long as the teachers are not stringing the students along for financial or egotistical goals.

---

[1] Interview with Papaji. http://www.firehorse.com.au/philos/papaji/

There are authentic teachers who are interested in helping others recognize their true nature. Many have come across gurus, teachers and authors who appear to be able to manipulate reality and have fantastic abilities and experiences. These individuals may or may not be enlightened, as you will come to understand later. These abilities and experiences are not indications of enlightenment. They serve only to embolden the ego of the doer, as they are able to manipulate the dream far beyond the ability of others. If they are not aware that they are only manipulated the dream then they are not enlightened. Some may be enlightened and have the ability to manipulate the dream. This is a tougher row to hoe, as the attention to the dream strengthens the artificial ego, making it more difficult to recognize your true self.

The purpose of this material is to point you in the right direction for you to awaken and to stay awake. Reaching recognition will require a straightforward and systematic approach. This material employs an approach that moves from one simple concept to another, until you reach the non-conceptual knowingness.

Amazingly Simple

It is simple, and it has been in front of you, around you, and in you all along. It is right there. Do you not see it? You are moments in a lifetime away from seeing It, knowing It, and becoming It. Once you understand it, you will never be the same again. You will unconditionally know it is the truth. No faith or belief is necessary.

What is There to Get?

Jesus said, "I shall give you what eyes have not seen,
what ears have not heard, what hands have not touched,
what has not come upon the human heart."

Gospel of Saint Thomas (17)

You are going to get a non-compromising, unshakable, beyond belief, understanding of the One, The That, the I AM, the Rapture, The Mystery of the universe, God. This is what you truly are, what you have always been, and always will be. If you have been seeking self-realization, enlightenment, God, your purpose then, this is it. If that is not enough then read no further.

Why should I want to Get This?

The finding of God is the coming to one's own self.

Meber Baba

Why should you want to get it? You should want to "get it" if you want to be one with God, remove suffering, to know what transcends death, to know without doubt who and what you really are. You will find out what is real and what is illusion.

A human's greatest desire is to realize their true self. It will relieve you of the burden of the search and the constant striving for perfection and correctness before God and yourself. You will find out that you are worthy and ready to recognize your enlightenment. That is why you are reading this book. You will find a simple happiness in life that previously eluded you. You will learn that you have nothing to worry about or fear anymore.

It will not be a state of unending bliss, but you can become aware of it and make it more your natural or resting state. Things will be different, but maybe not in the way you have always preconceived it to be.

The Milestones

The main milestone is for you to absolutely, non-conceptually know 24/7, without any doubt, that you as an individual do not exist; you never have and never will. You must rid yourself of the limiting I-thought. This is the thought that you are a separate and distinct individual. The dissolution of the I-thought will bring you Samadhi, the state of pure non-dualistic consciousness. You are fully realized right now. You are the ONE, all of IT. There is no other, No separation, no two. You are Nothingness, and Everything. You are eternal, indestructible, immutable, Intelligence Energy. You are free and aware now. The content of your awareness has nothing to do with the awareness itself. You are free to be happy, sad, tired, alive, awake and asleep. It is primarily a matter of perspective, focus, and resolution. If you look closely enough at the fabric of the illusion, you will see the reality close up and personal. Relax and enjoy the show.

The Challenges

As mentioned earlier, language and semantics are limited, as are the imperfect analogies and examples used to illustrate certain concepts. Since the milestones include non-conceptual knowledge, it seems strange that we need to understand concepts. At this point, you may be thinking that this is new age doublespeak.

The Key

The non-conceptual understanding of your non-duality and existence as Awareness is where the Awakening happens. It is otherwise just a collection of some very interesting concepts, but do not allow you to shift consciousness.

What is Advaita?

Advaita is the name of this line of thought and it is not new. It is at least 5000 years old. It is not doublespeak and it will make sense in the right context. It will all come together soon. Advaita is defined by Britanica as follows:

> (Sanskrit: "Nondualism," or "Monism"), most influential of the schools of Vedānta, an orthodox philosophy of India. While its followers find its main tenets already fully expressed in the Upaniṣads and systematized by the Vedānta-sūtras, it has its historical beginning with the 7th-century thinker Gauḍapāda, author of the Māṇḍūkya-kārikā, a commentary in verse form on the late Māṇḍūkya Upaniṣad.
>
> Gauḍapāda builds further on the Mahāyāna Buddhist philosophy of Śūnyavā-da ("Emptiness"). He argues that there is no duality; the mind, awake or dreaming, moves through maya ("illusion"); and only nonduality (advaita) is the final truth. This truth is concealed by the ignorance of illusion. There is no becoming, either of a thing by itself or of a thing out of some other thing. There is ultimately no individual self or soul (jiva), only the atman (all-soul), in which individuals may be temporarily delineated just as the space in a jar delineates a part of main space: when the jar is broken, the individual space becomes once more part of the main space.[2]

Advaita comes from ancient, 5000-year-old Indian Sanskrit texts. It is a Vedantic philosophy found in a collection of writings called the Upanishads. The word Advaita, means "not two" or "without duality". It is pronounced (ad-vī'ta) by

[2] **Advaita.** (2008). Encyclopædia

Britannica. *Britannica World Religions.*

Chicago: Encyclopædia Britannica.

most westerners. We will also use the term non-duality interchangeably.

Ancient Vedanta scholars in India first wrote about Advaita philosophy in about 3000 BC and they probably developed it about 1000 years earlier. As you will see later, time has no relevance to knowledge or anything else. Nonetheless, when most people hear of anything that is new to them and it varies from their prevailing viewpoints, they often are quick to ridicule. They may label it as new age whack or at least a cult, so be judicious with whom you share your new knowledge with. You should be able to tell those who are open to recognizing their own enlightenment.

Although Advaita comes from some of the oldest written texts known to man, the modern interpretations and their presentations are relatively new. The original translations are difficult to understand and assimilate. This material will not go into detail about the origins of Advaita, as there is plenty of that available elsewhere.

There are three main paths of Advaita, the traditional, direct path, and Neo-Advaita. In my opinion, the traditional path for most westerners is almost incomprehensible and frustrating at best. It is very abstract, seems contradictory, and leaves most wondering what they are supposed to do with these ideas. How do I apply them? How do I reach enlightenment? When I look back at it now, it all makes sense and seems extremely valid, but still from the point of view of a newcomer it looks impossible.

The Direct Path and Neo-Advaita are both relatively new approaches to Advaita and provide much more relevancy for most in this modern era. However, the Neo-Advaitan approach for me is not comprehensive enough to understand or to know what to do with the knowledge. It seems significantly more difficult to me to make the transition from conceptual to non-conceptual knowledge using this approach alone.

The approach employed here is mostly the Direct Path. This path will point you directly to look at yourself and conduct self-inquiries so that you can directly access and attain the knowledge you need to recognize your enlightenment. You will not see lengthy expositions about the experiences of myself or others or what it is like to be enlightened.

In the end, these different approaches are all just labels. These labels attempt to put different approaches into neat little boxes where they do not entirely fit. My assumption is that you are more interested in obtaining your own enlightenment than living vicariously through the enlightenment of others. The most important thing is that you get the understanding, no matter what the approach or label put on it.

Whatever you do, do not focus too much on picking apart the semantics, as these semantics are all disposable once you get the non-conceptual understanding. The concepts will not help you get any further beyond the point of recognition since there are no levels of enlightenment recognition. You either recognize it or you do not. The concepts will only help you get there.

Chapter 2

ORGANIC REALITY

To see the world in a grain of sand and heaven in a wild flower Hold infinity in the palm of your hand and eternity in an hour

Michael Talbot

The interpretation of the data collected by our five senses is what we perceive as organic reality on a day-to-day basis. In addition, we use technology such as glasses, hearing aids, telescopes, microscopes, stethoscopes, and other devices to enhance our ability. Our sense of reality all comes down to what our senses collect and how our brains/minds interpret the data. We see, hear, taste, touch, smell, and think. We discuss, teach, and come to collective consensus as to what is real and what is not. Our children reinforce these accepted models of reality from the day they are born until adulthood. We first teach our children that they are separate individuals with individual identities and even label them with semi-unique names.

In 1976, the evolutionary theorist Richard Dawkins coined the term **meme**, which describes units of cultural knowledge. Memes mutate, propagate and go extinct similar to organisms in nature. People collectively agree upon and accept these memes as units of reality within a culture, or micro-culture. There are many cultural constructs ranging in size from global, continental, national, regional, state, city, village, church, family, to individual. They overlap and intersect to form a unique collection of personal memes and that makeup our individual interpretation of reality.

Memes follow the same laws of natural selection as organisms do in species variation. They are constantly evolving and mutating. Those mutations that make the beliefs stronger are the ones that survive. There used to be a meme that said the earth was flat. That meme eventually became extinct, because it could not hold up to scrutiny. It tried to mutate into something survivable by those clinging onto the idea that it was a conspiracy to makes us believe the earth is round.

The field of medicine is another good example of how memes mutate, become extinct or become stronger. One of the common methods of treatment, back in the day, was to bleed the patient. Doctors would cut their patients and allow them to bleed a certain amount before closing the wound. Both the patients and those in the medical profession agreed and believed that this was helpful.

A memeplex is a collection of related memes. Memeplexes also have a life of their own. They are like self-sustaining organisms that exist to serve and preserve themselves. The successful mutations will define how they will evolve.

Our meme training begins when we first enter the world. Our minds fill themselves with our own unique collection of memes and memeplexes. In the first few days, we begin to accept the memes such as, I have a name, I am separate from other people and other objects, and the world is here to serve me.

Subscribing and unsubscribing to memes goes on throughout your entire life. You subscribe to a Santa Claus meme when you are a child and you unsubscribe to that meme when you are older. There is a sex is bad meme when you are young and there is a sex is good meme when you are married as an adult. People considered smoking healthful until the surgeon general publicly denounced it. The tobacco memeplex is very resilient, and has mutated in useful ways for its own survival. According to whether you are fundamentalist Christian or not, you may believe the meme that God created the earth in seven days, or that it was a result nature. They are both memes that inhabit the same space.

There is sometimes room for more than one meme or memeplex in the same niche as well. In any event, all humans identify with thousands of these memes and memeplexes and they become real for each of us. Our own unique intersection of memeplexes determines our perception of reality. We are in essence, the passive hosts to these parasitic pests that are using us in our ignorant bliss to keep them alive.

These memes and memeplexes were necessary for our early survival. If you wanted to challenge these in days gone by, you would do so at your own peril as many of the great visionaries in our history who have ever questioned the status quo. These people were known during their times as crackpots, heretics, and infidels by those who zealously held onto their cherished memes. Some went a step further and felt it was their personal mission to ensure everyone conformed to their memes as well. This intolerance is still alive and well today. The main point is that memes are powerful, self-sustaining, and adaptable. They will strongly resist denial or any attempts to drive them to extinction. Memes and memeplexes are what put flesh on the bones of our collective perceived reality.

If you are not able to consider any reality outside of your current view, then these ideas may not be right for you. You must be ready and open for the possibility that your current understanding of reality may not be correct.

"So God created man in his own image."

Genesis

Stop reading for a moment and look at the things around you now. What do you see? You can pick out lots of things. You see objects and put labels on them like, book, table, chair, husband, child, Bob, Mary, etc. In fact, when I asked you to look around you probably did exactly that; you began to mentally catalog what you saw as individual things. You probably did not think, "I see light waves bouncing off matter." You probably saw multiple occurrences of separation and individual things.

When you look at your hands you may say, "I see my hands." Then ask yourself, "What composes the hands?" You may say, "Skin, muscle, tendons, bones, nerves, etc." What composes the tissues of these items? You may answer "cells." What composes the cells? You would say, "Molecules." And what composes the molecules? You would say, "Atoms." And atoms are made of what? You would say, "Subatomic particles, like electrons, protons, and neutrons" Science has gone even further, but for illustration purposes, this is far enough.

We could go through this exercise on any kind of matter regardless of what the size or appearance, from a grain of sand to the largest planets and suns in the universe and we would get down to atoms and their subatomic particles. What your eyes are really doing is collecting light energy that bounces off these subatomic particles. The mind-brain interprets the nerve pulses originating from the light-energy striking the eye. Likewise, the ears are detecting sound wave energy. The other senses are also interacting with other forms of energy and subatomic particles

When we look closer at an atom we find that it is mostly empty space. In fact, let us look at a hydrogen atom. It is one ten millionth of a millimeter in diameter. The proton in the middle is a thousand times smaller. The electron is thousand times smaller than the proton.

If you scaled a proton to the size of a basketball, an electron would be about the size of the head of a pin. The distance between the proton and electron would be about eleven miles in a hydrogen atom. That is about 99.9% empty space in an typical atom. The universe has slightly more empty space if even if you consider planets and stars as solid; which they are not.

The nature of the subatomic particles is peculiar as well. Modern science has discovered that they are sort everywhere and only in one place in their orbit at the same time. When you observe them, their behavior and characteristics change. They are not solid. They are energy. These subatomic particles are the common substrate of the entire universe that the Sanskrit texts refer to as Brahman, the One, the Self, God. We will come back to this concept later.

Holographic Universe: Our Recursive Reality

Jesus saw some little ones nursing. He said to his disciples, "These little ones who are nursing resemble those who enter the kingdom." They said to him, "So shall we enter the kingdom by being little ones? "Jesus said to them, "When you make the two one and make the inside like the outside and the outside like the inside and the above like the below, and that you might make the male and the female be one and the same, so that the male might not be male nor the female be female, when you make eyes in place of an eye and a hand in place of a hand and a foot in place of a foot, an image in place of an image - then you will enter the kingdom.

Gospel of Saint Thomas (22)

As it is above, it is below. The universe is a homogenous sea of mostly empty space and billions of galaxies. It is one thing, a sea of nothingness and energy. The galaxies are mostly empty space and solar systems. The solar systems are mostly empty space, stars, planets and other matter-energy bodies. Our earth is made of mostly empty space matter-energy bodies and large organisms. The large organisms are populated with billions of cells, some, as parts of tissues, some as free agents, like blood cells, bacteria, nematodes, and other microbes. The cells and microbes are also made of nucleuses, mitochondria, and other bodies. It all goes on and on down to the subatomic particles. They all appear to be collections of independent and individual objects. The repeating patterns and the similarity of our universe make it appear to be holographic and recursive all the way down to the atomic structure. Where an independent thing begins and ends seems to be quite fuzzy.

Emptiness Everywhere

We detect vibrations of energy with our sight, touch, and hearing and particles of energy-matter when we taste and smell. The senses convert their inputs into to energy in the form of nerve transmissions to the brain. Our senses are detectors and transmitters of energy. Our mind-brains act as our sixth sense. The synergy of the five senses and emotion synthesize our perception of organic reality. Even though we are detecting energy that appears to be solid, it is all mostly empty space from the universe down to the subatomic particles. If you look closely enough at reality, you will see it is made of a common substrate of mostly empty space and energy.

If you have a gold ring and melt it down all you will have is gold. You can melt and recast the gold into a cross. You can melt the cross and you will have gold again. The same goes with the organic reality, whatever it is, if you melt it down it is just the substrate underneath no matter what form it has taken on.

Chapter 3

MAYA THE ILLUSION

His disciples said to him, "When is the kingdom going to come?" Jesus said, "It is not by being waited for that it is going to come. They are not going to say, 'Here it is' or 'There it is.' Rather, the kingdom of the father is spread out over the earth, and people do not see it."

Gospel of Saint Thomas (113)

Maya is the term used in the ancient Sanskrit writings of Indian to describe the illusion of what we know to be organic reality. As the old saying goes, "seeing is believing." On the other hand, is it? We are detecting energy when we use our senses and translating into nerve impulses for our mind-brains to interpret. Our interpretations are not reality. They are thoughts. They are illusions, like your sleeping dreams are illusions.

Have you ever thought upon awakening, that anything within the dream was real? Did you feel bad for the person running from the tiger in your dream, once you were awake?

Of course not, because there never was a tiger or this character. They were not real. They were illusions. Even if the tiger were chasing after your character in the dream, would you still be afraid that he would catch and eat you, once awake? Of course not, you would say, "It was just a dream and even though I am still shaking with fear, I know it can't hurt me. It is not real. It felt real at the time, but I know it is not real now because I woke up."

This waking illusion of Maya is not like any other illusion you have ever experienced including sleeping dreams. Nonetheless, sleeping dreams do make good, if not flawed analogy. The waking illusion validates itself on many levels as real. It stands up to scrutiny. It is robust, complex, resilient, and tough. It has endless levels of complexity that can be explored and investigated by science and thought. It is multi-dimensional and our science and quantum physics are pushing the limits of knowledge further every day. We call the laws that of govern this illusion the laws of physics, at least the ones that pertain to Newtonian Physics. There are now other discoveries, which have added more laws to the mix, which go beyond Newtonian physics into the realm of quantum physics. This leaves us with almost infinite levels of detail and complexity in the organic reality to poke, prod, and convince us that it is true.

The sleeping dream has no rules, and anything goes. These dreams have little definition and are flimsy. If it were not for the narcotic stupor we occupy while sleeping, we would easily become aware that we are dreaming. Lucid dreaming is this state of awareness within the dream.

Some mystics have claimed to achieved remarkable feats or demonstrated levels of knowledge within organic reality that seem to defy the laws of physics or at least go well beyond what most can imagine possible. They report fantastic and mystical experiences that happen within the organic reality or beyond. As fantastic as these experiences and abilities appear, they are still happening within the illusion of organic reality or waking illusion.

Classical Enlightenment, or enlightenment as most commonly understood, does not exist outside the illusion. It occurs within the illusion, but appears to go beyond the bounds of what we believe to be possible in organic reality. Nonetheless, The Waking illusion also referred to as organic reality is awesome. Enjoy it, but know it for what it really is; a dream.

The movie The Matrix depicted an analogues illusion to our organic world illusion. The main character awoke to the dream and found out that what he thought was real was all an illusion. In this film, most people never came close to figuring out that their reality was a dream except for the elite. Unfortunately, the actual reality was not nearly as comfortable and pleasant as their dream reality, as another race was using their bodies as electronic batteries. The main character had to choose to take a red or a blue pill. He would awaken from the dream if he took one of the pills. The main character knew that if he did take the pill that would wake him up, he could never be ignorant of true reality again. This is similar to what you are about to do now. There is no turning back once you know the truth.

Our sleeping dreams are dreams within the dream of our waking reality is an example of how our reality is recursive, that is within one illusion is contained another. When we awaken within the sleeping dream we realize it is a dream and not real. We also need to awaken to our organic reality. As we call the awakened state within the sleeping dream, Lucid Dreaming, we can call the awakened state within the organic reality, Lucid Wakefullness.

The Ego

For it is easier for a camel to go through a needle's eye, than for a rich man to enter into the kingdom of God.
LUKE 18:25

Self-identification roles as I am a mother, I am an accountant, I am rich, I am poor, and I am a catholic, are all extensions of the ego. These sorts of identifications come from your back-story or history. Physical characteristics as I am black, I am white, I am tall, I am old are also extensions to the ego. There are other attributes as I am beautiful, young, strong, and others that will change as you age. People who carry the burden of having exceptional attributes in this category find it much more difficult to let go of their ego, because they have desirable aspects of ego that they are not willing to give up these things that makes them feel in some superior. Ego loves superior.

That which changes is not real. Beauty, youth, and physical prowess will all diminish with time. When the body dies everything else of the illusory self that the ego identifies with will also die. It is all an illusion. Ownership of physical objects and status in society are all part of ego.

The ego is a packrat that hordes everything it can to make itself appear bigger, better, and more desirable. The ego desires to be the envy of all other egos, to be the best ego ever. An ego detests losing any aspect of itself that makes it strong. This can be either negative or positive aspects. Some egos or built upon a negative back-story, like I had a tough upbringing, I was abused, I was poor or they may have had a positive back-story such as I was the Prom Queen, I am famous celebrity, and so forth. The positive back-stories are by far the hardest to let go of since these are desirable and make your life easier. A negative back-story may give you an incentive to seek awakening, but they may also serve as crutch or excuse not to seek it. In either event, these back-stories or other ways of forming our self-identity are part of what makes our egos whole and makes them strong.

Me, Myself, and I

When you make a statement about yourself, as, "I do not think I am worthy of becoming enlightened, there are two different entities in this sentence. The first I is making a judgment upon the second I. How about the statement, "I do not feel well?" Who is not feeling well? Who observed the one not feeling well? Who are all these people anyway? There are at least two I's always present. There is only one I that is real. There are not two, only the One. The unreal one is ego and it is make believe. It is a dream.

Your mind is the world of the ego and your awareness the world of the true you. You need to loose, forget, or ignore your mind to awakening.

Understand that the path to enlightenment is the severance of your identification from your ego, such that you no longer have an ego. There may be one present and hanging around, but you are separate from it. You will no longer be at the mercy of your ego or the rest of the Maya anymore.

Not Asking You to Believe

Jesus said, "Whatever you hear with your ear, proclaim upon your rooftops into the other ear. Indeed, no one lights a lamp and puts it under a vessel, nor puts it in a hidden place Rather it is put on a lamp stand so that each who enters and leaves might see its light."

Gospel of Saint Thomas (33)

You may be thinking about now that this all sounds great and that I am asking you to believe my interpretation of reality; Nope, not at all. I do not think you should ever believe anything anyone tells you at face value. They may be dead wrong even though they may believe it with every fiber in their body. Check it out for yourself.

Upon awakening you will no longer say, "I 100% believe or I believe with all my heart that such and such is true." You will no longer need to believe anything. Beliefs are the glue that holds the fabric of Maya together.

These first three chapters are mental preparation for you to come to your own conclusions. Think of everything up until this point as theory that you will use to prove or disprove your awareness of what you truly are. My goal is to go beyond conceptual knowledge to non-conceptual knowingness that is a state of knowing within you that is beyond question. I am not talking about belief or faith. Neither of these concepts will be necessary. Think of all of this as necessary mental preparation for the journey you are going to conduct now. This is not going to happen in some distant future after years of discipline practice. Your flowering is going to happen in the here and the now. You are on the precipice of transforming your life forever.

Chapter 4

PULL AWAY THE VEILS

Let's Investigate

"Your natural state has no relationship whatsoever with the religious states of bliss, beatitude and ecstasy; they lie within the field of experience. Those who have led man on his search for religiousness throughout the centuries have perhaps experienced those religious states. So can you. They are thought-induced states of being, and as they come, so do they go. Krishna Consciousness, Buddha Consciousness, Christ Consciousness, or what have you, are all trips in the wrong direction: they are all within the field of time. The timeless can never be experienced, can never be grasped, contained, much less given expression to, by any man. That beaten track will lead you nowhere. There is no oasis situated yonder; you are stuck with the mirage."

It is interesting to note that the preceding excerpt from U.G. Krishnamurti, a self-realized individual who reported major, significant physical and biological changes upon his self-realization. He identified these as experiences that were unique to him and that all experiences are unique to individuals. He further explained that experiences all occurred within the illusion of organic reality.

If you are not ready for the truth, go no further. This is your last warning, because this truth will shatter your belief system. Most of what you currently believe as truth will dissolve. You may be reluctant to give up some of these old beliefs at first, because your ego still wants them to be true. You have personally invested your trust in these beliefs and they will not die easily. Nonetheless, the truth of your actual reality is unavoidable once you examine it. You will not be trading one set of beliefs for another, as this is not about beliefs.

You should neither anticipate nor seek experiences for the sake of enlightenment, because if you are seeking experiences you are seeking within the illusion. This is not where you will find your True Self.

As you explore and discover what is not true, you will see that what is left is that which is true. It is the only thing left, the True Self, the One, The Brahman, God. This is the Substrate, the Everything and the No Thing. This Intelligence-Energy is pure Awareness. It can only be Aware of what it is and that is Itself. The illusion is also the Brahman. The Observer is the Brahman and the Observed is the Brahman. There is only One. If you look at the illusion close enough you will see that the fabric of the illusion is the Brahman, the One.

---

[3] Krishnamurti, U.G., The Mystique of Enlightenment. *Compiled by James Brodsky from conversations in India and Switzerland 1973.* http://www.well.com/user/jct/Mystique.htm

When you look at the illusion close enough it all gets down to the same thing, a whole bunch of empty space and non-matter energy of sub atomic particles. This substrate is homogenous and it is the ONE. In the last few years, our science has begun to detect the One. Human senses have poor resolution. Think about how the earth appears when viewed from outer space. Awesome beautiful yes, but without the details we see every day. Even farther out it would appear as a mere speck of dim light or only detectable as a small gravity well. When you drill down to the micro level you will observe the same phenomenon, things look a whole lot different but a whole lot the same as outer space. It is all mostly empty space and at the atomic level, there is nothing solid.

Why do you identify with only parts of the substrate? Why do you not identify with this book you are currently holding? It is as much you as is your body. It is all just a continuum of the sea of wave energy. Is a wave in the ocean separate from the ocean itself? Should a wave identify with only its transitory existence or is it a temporary swirling of the energy of the ocean. Is it not the ocean? We need to investigate in order to answer these questions and move from intellectual knowledge to non-conceptual knowledge.

I am not important. My experiences are not important, and everyone else's experiences are not important. Myself, you, Jesus, Krishna, Buddha, and the dust floating in the air at this moment are all of equal and no importance. No guru, teacher, Saint, Savior, or any homeless person lying in the street is any better, more advanced or more saintly than you. The only difference is whether they or you non-conceptually know themselves to be enlightened.

You can gain non-conceptual understanding instantaneously. It will take some direction on where and how to look.

Do you see it yet? It is right there. It has always been available to you. You are so close to recognizing your own enlightenment that you may even laugh with surprise and joy about how close you have always been.

You came to believe you were a separate person from your childhood programming. You are not separate from anything. This book can teach you nothing. It can point you in the right direction. Show you where to look and what questions to ask yourself. You are the real teacher and the student. I know, this sounds like New Age doubletalk, but stay with it and it will become clear.

When I was a young boy, I used to think that everyone else around me was an animated robot, artificial persons who lived on this earth for the purpose of my experiences. It was as if I were living in a movie. I believed I was the only real person and others were here for my benefit. I now know that I was partially right all along. I was right concerning the others not being real. They are all not real, nor am I. We are here for our own benefit, but there is no we. There is only the One. I was close to understanding even as a young child, but I accepted the memes of our society and quickly discarded those ideas as mere fanciful thoughts.

As a child, I was frequently in the state of Lucid Wakefullness. Alas, I fell back asleep into the dream of organic reality for many decades. I struggled to awaken again by seeking enlightenment during the many decades that followed. I knew it was all a dream but I could not figure out how to wake up. I am thrilled that I was able to awaken once again and this time it is for good.

What is it About?

> Jesus said, "when you make the two into one you will become sons of man, and when you say, 'O mountain, go elsewhere!' it will go elsewhere."
>
> Gospel of Saint Thomas (33)

You are eventually going to understand that you, your mind, your ego, and your body does not exist. It is an illusion and you are not a separate identity. You will acquire a non-conceptual knowingness that it is true. This is not an intellectual knowing, but a real absolute conviction that it is true. You can do this by proving it to yourself. This is not something that will happen in some distant future. It can only happen in the here in the now.

Who is the Doer?

> I am not absent-minded. It is the presence of mind that makes me unaware of everything else.
>
> G.K. Chesterton

Are your ears hearing and your eyes seeing? No, they are not. They are organic instruments receiving energy and transmitting their reactions through the nervous system to the brain. The brain interprets the signals and formulates thoughts. The brain also is an instrument, and it does not hear or see. When the body dies, the body does not hear, see, touch, taste or smell nor do the sensory organs themselves. The body never could see or hear the world, as the body is a receiver, translator, and transmitter. It is not the recipient of the seeing and hearing. When it dies, it can no longer even detect energy.

Discover who and what you are by the negation of what you are not. Once you discard what you are not, what is left is what you are. You must discard what you are not as you would shuck away the husk of an ear of corn to reveal the beautiful kernels beneath. Discard what you are not, to reveal the shining, ever-present self that remains. This immutable Self cannot be burned by fire, cut by a sword or harmed in any way.

Four Principal Totalities

Neither shall they say, Lo here! or, lo there! for, behold,
the kingdom of God is within you.

LUKE 17:21

You must use your mind and the Maya to prove to
yourselves that the mind, the Maya and "The me" do not exist.
Do not take my word for it. Investigate it for yourself.

If I tell you that seawater is not blue, do not take my word
for it, find out for yourself. Know with absolute certainty that
seawater is not blue. You will never question this again. The
same thing goes for organic reality and your perception of
yourself. Investigate your mind-body and see if this is you.
Once you know it is not, you will never have to question this
again.

The following four absolute philosophic concepts, also
known as totalities, are the most powerful tools of
enlightenment. It may take repeated investigations of these
totalities to solidify your awakening. If you get one, that is, the
non-conceptual, gut level, unshakable understanding, you will
get the others. You will know you are the One and it is
irreversible. Any one of these could give you the revelation.
Get one and the others will fall into place.

1. Look for the Me

Every cell in your body replaces itself on a regular basis,
in intervals no more than around a few years. Do you believe
that any cells of your body are the same as they were 10
years ago? Is this body you have today the true you, or is the
body of 10 years ago. Since your body is always changing
and your sense of you does not seem to change at all, it is
apparent that you are not your body. Your preferences have
changed, your body has changed, and many other things
have changed, but your sense of yourself, that which has a
body and a mind, has not changed.

Is your mind, the same thing as it was 10 years ago, 10 months ago, 10 days ago, 10 seconds ago? Your mind is in a constant state of change and it changes at breakneck speed. It only takes the time for neuro-pathways to form and electronic impulse to travel across them. In fact, science has recently discovered that the brain has quality called neuroplasticity[4]. This allows the brain to physically grow and create additional brain pathways structure well into old age by exercising the brain through intellectual pursuits. Clearly, your brain is always changing. Your brain and mind is something you occupy and use, but is not you.

Is your ego the true you or is your ego a collection of thoughts and memories? Your ego is artificial and delusional in that it thinks it is real. It spends its illusory existence trying to validate its own reality. The ego is a construct of the mind, like a computer-programmed Avatar that you can find in video games or virtual reality worlds like Second Life on the internet.

Your body, mind and ego are all ever changing. If these are not real, what is left? The true you, the never changing True Self, which is the One, the only thing that is, the I am. The You that is timeless, changeless, ageless, and immortal. There is no separation between what you believe yourself to be in the organic world and any other thing, person, entity, rock, mineral, ray of light or God. It is all part of the whole, the substrate, the One, the I am, like a wave in the ocean is not separate from the ocean. The wave is merely a different organization of the energy in the ocean, but all is part of the whole ocean. It is all one. There is no duality, no divisions, no two, only the One and the Infinite.

That which is left is what you feel yourself to be, that which makes you know that you exist. It is the awareness of your true self, the awareness of the illusion, your body, your mind, and your ego. It is that which never changes and is always observing. You are the Awareness, not your body,

---

4 Peterson, Richard, *Inside the Investor's Brain*. John Wiley and Sons, Inc. 2007

mind, or ego. You are not the contents of the awareness, but the Awareness itself. The content is the illusion.

If the preceding paragraphs did not fully resonate, read it slowly again right now, until you completely comprehend it.

Whenever you begin to doubt the reality of your true nature or how you came to this understanding reread "Look for the me" section again. It may take you one or two times or maybe more. Once you have the non-conceptual knowing about who and what you are, it will stick with you. You will need to do this exercise only until you get to the point that you know it 24/7. Not that you need to think about it 24/7, but keep it under the surface, as you know that when the clouds block the sun, that the sun is still there. You cannot go back; you will never again think that the seawater is blue or that you are a separate entity again.

You may think that you feel you exist. Let me clarify. Repeat after me, "I, insert name here, do not exist. Me, the real me absolutely does exist."

2. Time is Not Real

When you sit with a nice girl for two hours, you think it's only a minute. But when you sit on a hot stove for a minute, you think it's two hours. That's relativity.

Albert Einstein

Time does not exist. Science has proven this. It sure seems like it exists. After spending an entire lifetime looking at clocks, making appointments, reporting to work or school on a schedule, it is somewhat hard not to believe that it exists. After all, one of the primary behaviors that indicate you are a maturing person is that you can make it to work or school on time. The illusion strongly supports the concept that time exists. How else could you age or get to tomorrow if there was not any time? Does your dog or cat know or think about time? They all have memories, but no sense of time.

There is only the here and the now, no future, no past. If this is difficult to understand, be patient as the illusion is strong and it reinforces itself continuously.

Have you ever been aware in the past? No, the past is a memory in the present moment. Memories are thoughts. Have you ever been aware in the future? No, the future also is a thought in the present moment. What is left? The here and the now is left, no past, no future. This is the only time and place that you can ever be or be aware of. You are only aware in the here and the now. Time appears to elapse but it does not. Your awareness is in the here and the now only. Your awareness is what you are.

When does a moment start and stop? It never starts and it never stops. It is continuous and not discrete. It is only right here and right now. There is no other logical conclusion than time does not exist. To non-conceptually understand is difficult for many, but give it time, it will settle in.

The advantage of a bad memory is that one enjoys
several times the same good thing for the first time.

Friedrich Nietzsche

It isn't so astonishing, the number of things that I can
remember, as the number of things I can remember that
aren't so.

Mark Twain

*I have a remarkable memory, I forget everything. It is
wonderfully convenient. It is though the world were
constantly renewing itself.*

Jules Renard

3. Free Will

> All the activities that the body performs are
> predetermined. The only freedom you have is to choose
> not to identify with the body that is performing the action.
>   Sri Poonja (Papaji)[5]

The only free will you have is the choice to identify yourself with your body/mind/ego or with the Pure Awareness that you are.

Try to stop all thought. Unless you are a very experienced meditator you will probably find this difficult, nonetheless, notice that when the thoughts do appear, they come out of nowhere. They just appear. Do you choose to have happy, sad, or angry thoughts? Do these thoughts appear as the result of observances and thoughts that preceded them?

Let us say that I threw a pebble and hit you in the head. There will be thoughts that will arise which you have no control over. You might think something like, "You bastard! You hit me in the head for no reason, it hurts and I am mad." Did you choose to have those thoughts or did they come up on their own? Now you might say, "I have been meditating and controlling my mind for years and I would not have those thoughts." You are probably right, but you would have other thoughts come up spontaneously. You may even be able to predict what they would be, but you would not decide when and what they would be. All actions and experiences result from the thoughts and actions that preceded them, as far back as you want to go. What you think about this moment is a result of a chain of events that goes all the way back to your childhood. Since each action or though is the deterministic result of the ones that preceded they are all linked.

---

[5] Interview with Sri Poonja. http://sentient.org/past/poonja.html

Your ego will take credit and claim ownership on every thought or action. The ego will say, "I originated that thought." The ego does not originate any thought or action. It takes credit and ownership to validate its existence. Make no mistake about it, your ego is a survivor and will do whatever it takes to convince you that it is real and does exist.

All our actions and thoughts are deterministic. What this means is that current actions or thoughts are determined by the thoughts and actions that preceded them. This chain of actions and thoughts goes all the way back to your birth. You are what you are because of the experiences, thoughts and actions that occurred in your life and what you do next is predetermined by that history. It does not mean that no matter what you do or think that the results will be the same.

Lack of free will is not the same thing as an inescapable fate. Fate implies that it does not matter what happens before an event, action, or thought and that the results will always be the same no matter what precedes it. Not having free will or "no free will" implies that what has happened before will determine the outcome of future events, actions and thoughts.

You may think that it still feels as if you have free will, that you are free to think or do anything you want. Do you choose your thoughts? Do not your thoughts bubble up from nowhere? One thought spawns another. Thoughts such as, I am thirsty and I will get a drink are predetermined. Did you choose to think you were thirsty?

The Bill Murray character in Ghost Busters beautifully demonstrated this phenomenon by his inability to choose his thoughts. He could not stop from thinking of the Marshmallow Man when asked to choose the course of his own destruction by the demon. Moments after the demon declares that they would choose their course, a giant marshmallow man strolls onto the screen. The Bill Murray character says, "I couldn't help it. It just came into my head."

Should criminals and wrong doers, be held accountable since they too have no free will? The police and the judges also have no free will so they will do what they do and catch and convict the criminal. The poor hapless non-existent criminal must suffer, but the reality is that the criminal is not real. No one suffered, only the illusion occurred. When you leave the movie theater, do you feel sorry for the characters locked up in prison or even put to death? No, you will not feel for them, because they are not real.

If you do not accept all of the previous discussion about free will, ask yourself who is the me, who is the doer, who does or does not have free will. You, your ego, does not exist as a separate entity; there is nobody to have free will.

You may ask, "If there is no free will, why not become a serial killer?" You can no more choose to become a serial killer than Jeffrey Dalmer could choose not to be one. If you are a bank robber, you will rob banks; that is what you do. If you are not a bank robber you can no more will yourself to rob a bank than the bank robber can resist robbing the bank.

The Frog and the Scorpion

There is a Native American story about a scorpion and a frog. The scorpion walked up to the frog and asked him to carry him across the river. The frog said, "No, I will not carry you across the river because you will sting me and I will die." The scorpion replied, "That is nonsense, because if I sting you we will both sink and die." Therefore, the frog thought about it and agreed to carry the scorpion across the river.

About half way across the river, the scorpion stings the frog. The frog begins to lose control of his muscles and with his dying breath asks the scorpion why he stung him. The scorpion replied, "Because I am a scorpion."

4. Reincarnation

Reincarnation means to be made flesh again, that is, for the ego to reanimate in a new body. Since the ego-mind-body is not real, there is nothing to reincarnate. They all dissolve even when looking at them within the illusion. There is no self to reanimate in any new body. In the appearance or the illusion, you may say there is reincarnation, but even that is like one wave in the ocean morphing into another. Did one wave reincarnate into another or is the entire ocean moving about. What claim does the second wave have over the first? Is it the same thing reincarnated into another or is it all seawater?

Have you ever noticed that when most people say they are aware of their past lives, they either claim to have been famous or successful persons in their past lives? No one sees himself or herself in a past life as a mentally disturbed homeless person or a real bad person. There may be access to the memories or the thought of others that your mind identifies with and assumes was a past life. The ego would automatically claim that this is past life as this further serves to validate the reality of the ego.

You, the One, have always been free of the birth-death-rebirth cycle. There is nothing to reincarnate, because the ego is not real and the True You is nonmalleable, ever-present, and never changing. It is never born and it never dies. It is Awareness.

Significance of the Four Totalities

The non-conceptual understanding of the preceding four totalities is essential to making the shift in consciousness from the egocentric duality existence to the non-dualistic consciousness of Awareness. This shift in consciousness may happen rapidly and dramatically like an explosion of light and awareness upon your consciousness or it may happen gradually. Always come back to these four totalities until belief is no longer necessary, until you non-conceptually understand them.

Flip the Switch

If you understand and agree with the four principal totalities, but you just cannot seem to go the last mile of total non-conceptual understanding, here is the critical step.

You may have spent your entire life believing in or working on a set of basic beliefs and have probably committed a large amount of time and energy on them. You have huge investment in these beliefs. You may have created a very stringent discipline of what you must do and think to reach enlightenment or to be eligible to go to heaven. You may still be fearful or reluctant to drop these beliefs or routines. This is understandable considering how long and hard you worked on these beliefs.

On one hand, you now understand via the direct path of self-inquiry what you truly are and you have the ability to go back as many times as you like and re-verify it. On the other hand, you have read, studied, learned and evolved a certain set of ideas over your lifetime that you have come to accept on faith that must be true. You have not been able to validate these beliefs totally, but you have reinforced these from multiple sources over a lifetime. These are very powerful memes.

Look and re-look at the self-inquiries until you convince yourself that no matter how many times you look; they are not going to change. This is analogous to knowing that when a cloud drifts in front of the sun that the sun will still be there after the cloud passes. You do not have to check to see if the sun is still there anymore. It will take a great amount courage, but you must let the beliefs go in the face of the undeniable knowingness you now posses. Release yourself. You do not have to continue to believe. Let them go and set yourself free.

Chapter 5

AM I ENLIGHTENED YET?

The short answer is yes, if you choose to be. If you choose to give up those beliefs that prevent you from realizing your true self, beliefs, as I am not worthy, I am not special enough; I have not worked hard enough. You may also have beliefs such as I have worked very hard on developing the vision of God and heaven that I now have. I am not naive and I have spent years getting to where I am. I know I have had true spiritual experiences. Sorry, it is fantasy. The same fantasy I spent thirty years experiencing. That is a hard pill to swallow, but if you want to have true enlightenment that is what you must give up. There is no compromise. If you enjoy the fantasies better, stay with your fantasies.

The reality of true enlightenment is far superior to any fantasy. You will have to trust me on this until the full force of your self-awareness settles in, and you will know for yourself. An exciting experience in true life is much more satisfying than seeing one on the silver screen. Would you prefer to watch someone in a movie on a whitewater raft or ride down the river yourself? Would you prefer watching a couple onscreen have passionate sex or have it yourself? This analogy works from the organic reality illusion to true enlightenment as well. Hoping and having faith that enlightenment is going to be a certain way will not make it happen. It is what it is; embrace it.

If there is any doubt that your old beliefs are fantasies, go back to the four totalities, study them, ask yourself who was having all these great spiritual experiences? The one having these great spiritual experiences is a fantasy you in the fantasy illusion. These experiences are as real as the experiences in organic reality, which itself is an illusion. You must choose between beliefs and non-conceptual knowing.

If you understand the four totalities there is the one thing between you and your enlightenment is your refusal to let go of your fantasy beliefs. Beliefs are useful in the exploration of the illusion and they are an obstacle in attaining enlightenment as they make the illusion stronger and give it more complexity and texture.

The Conventional Phases of Enlightenment

Phase One: The Illusion within the Illusion

The Illusion within the illusion is that part of spiritual development that involves identifying with a huge memeplex of a religious point of view. In my case, it was the catholic religion. I was born into a catholic family and attended a catholic grade school. The catholic faith went back generations in my father's family, all the way back to Ireland when my Duffy family migrated to Indiana in the 1820s. The Catholic Church being the oldest Christian faith has roots all the way back to Peter, the first nominal Pope of the Catholic Church. Billions of people have been Christians throughout history, thousands of churches, hundreds of thousands if not millions of people work or have worked for the Christian churches. Billions of dollars every year support Christian churches. Millions of people believe with every fiber of their body that what the church tells them is manifest from God.

I developed in this memeplex. This was how I believed an enlightened person would appear. Jesus, Moses, the saints, the popes, and the scholars like Thomas Merton represented this ideal. All these people, all this money and all the years of devotion could not be wrong, could it?

When I went away to college, I was still going to church every Sunday until I took two classes in college that shattered the foundation of my Catholic memeplex. The first was a European history class where I discovered that the Catholic Church and most European governments were one in the same. It seemed that most of what the Catholic Church was trying to accomplish was to assert its power as governments do and had little to do with the spiritual development of its parishioner. Furthermore, I learned about the horrible crusades and other atrocities conducted against non-Christians including some of my other ancestors the Native Americans. If that wasn't enough I started questioning some of the modern day rules of the church, which to violate was a sin, like using no birth control in marriage and having as many children possible or abstaining from sex. I was several years away from getting married, but at nineteen years old, that did not seem quite right to me. Therefore, things were starting to look shaky on the Catholic front.

The second class I took was the history of Eastern Religions, the most interesting class I ever took through three college degrees. What fascinated me here were all these different interpretations of how to relate to God. In the case of most eastern religions it appeared that the main goal was not to have priest tell you what to do and how to live, but how one can develop their own personal and direct relationship with God and seek enlightenment while living on earth. This doctrine had no waiting for death as in the Catholic and other Christians churches, all the while wondering if you were good enough to make the cut. In addition, I began to wonder how you could go to hell or purgatory for eternity, for missing mass once in lifetime, harsh for a loving God.

I quit going to church and spent the next thirty plus years searching for enlightenment using eastern methods in an attempt to attain nirvana. You could change the above story to many other religions and the result may be about the same. The important point here is not my experience, because everybody's experiences are different, but that the only thing that kept me tied to the Catholic Church was faith or a belief that what the church was telling me would turn out to be true. I would find out that truth once I was deceased. The size, the infrastructure, the history, the power of the church made it all hard not to believe, but in the end it was a belief and I let go.

Phase Two: Growth

This phase lasted the longest for me, where I experimented with many different forms of meditation. These included several Eastern, Native American, and New Age forms of mediation all with varying degrees of success. I followed many teachers or Gurus for several years at a time, read and studied hundreds of books and meditated like a madman.

I made some spiritual progress but benefited more psychologically and physically because of the meditation. There was not anything to shake my foundation at this time, but the many incidents of scandal in the organized religions confirmed that I did not belong there. I also stopped drinking during this 29-year period as I felt it interfered with my spiritual development. Still I had no enlightenment and a few spiritual experiences.

Phase Three: Direct Experience in the Illusion

During the last four to five years of my thirty year period of searching, I began to intensify my quest by meditating twice a day and studying feverishly from several teachers. I began to make significant progress, as measured by dramatic spiritual experiences during my meditations. I believed I was at last nearing the end of my journey, as these experiences seemed as real as every day organic reality. It was during this period I began to re-look at non-duality as well and try to get my mind around this elusive state of knowingness described in many books and teachers. It all seemed believable and made sense but the transition from believing to non-conceptual knowingness eluded me in the beginning on this cognitive path to enlightenment.

It was soon after a meditation session that the light came on and I experienced my self-awareness for the first time. This turned out to be the easier part of what I now consider a two-part transition. The second part may be more difficult particularly if you dedicated a large part of your life on an intensive search for enlightenment and you have achieved significant spiritual experiences that seemed as real as the organic reality of everyday life.

The last statement encapsulates the difficulty and the solution to making the transition. Since the experiences were direct experiences and were not beliefs based on something heard or read, they were much stronger beliefs because of the connection to the physical body and mind. In addition, the personal investment in time, effort, money, and pride that brought me to this point made it much more difficult to let these beliefs go.

The solution has to do with the concept that the experiences resulting from the meditations were as real as organic reality. Since I had come to a non-conceptual understanding that organic reality was an illusion, what I had accomplished with my direct experiences was also part of the illusion. In a sense, I had made progress within the illusion of discovering even more of its complexity that not many have accomplished. In this dream of reality, I had accomplished something that tied me stronger to the illusion and strengthened my ego's self-identity as being real.

Phase Four: Direct Self Realization

To overcome this memeplex of a more advanced reality I repeatedly compared the fantasy and belief system of organic reality and the related spiritual experiences against the non-conceptual knowingness I had obtained. After doing this several times over several days, it became clear and unambiguous that my awakening was complete. The dropping of the last vestiges of my belief systems became inevitable and effortless in the end.

The steps that I took along my journey are common for many seekers of enlightenment, but are unnecessary. The reason I bring this up at all is to illustrate that this long and arduous path to enlightenment even makes it harder at the end, because you must overcome stronger attachment to the illusion, your ego and beliefs.

If you have not made these efforts at this point in your life, congratulations, your transition to self-awareness may be a lot easier.

It does not have to be difficult or arduous. You do not have be worthy by virtue of your hard work toward enlightenment, your purity of thought or action, or your saintly deeds on earth. These are parts of the illusion that distracts one from seeing the true you; it is all elegant and complex.

The Fast Track to Enlightenment

None of the steps of the conventional phases of enlightenment is necessary. Go straight to the brass ring. It is right in front of you and within your grasp. Skip all the years of searching, meditating, praying, studying and paying for enlightenment. If you are on the conventional path, cut your losses and stop; just say no. It is all a distraction, all part of the Maya or illusion of reality. You have looked at everything you need in order to become one with the non-conceptual knowingness of Everything and Nothing, all that there is, the One.

If the implications of what you have experienced do not shake the foundation of your perception of reality, go back and look at the Four Totalities once again. You have made a profound discovery about whom you really are, do not take it lightly and do not underestimate its ability to make positive change in your life and lives of those around you. This is probably radically different from any beliefs or pre-conceived notions of what you thought about reality. As has been emphasized several times in this book, beliefs are no longer necessary once you establish non-conceptual knowingness.

If you have a burning desire for enlightenment and self-realization this is your chance. If you are apathetic or curious go back to sleep now and live your life the same as always. The biggest opportunity of your life is knocking right now, in the present moment.

Saintliness Versus Enlightenment

When one becomes enlightened, does it follow that they become saintly in words and deeds? The answer is no, unless that is what they are going to do. Becoming aware of your enlightenment does not mean that you will begin leading the perfect life, because your ego, although changed and subdued is still a fictional character in a fictional land. A person aware of his or her own enlightened will change to a more detached, less emotionally driven, and less narcissistic being. The true you, your presence-awareness will realize that the ego is an illusion and the ego will not take itself as seriously as it has in the past. The ego has reluctantly revealed itself as fraud, poor ego.

There is a likelihood that an enlightened person becomes a better person as they realize that they do have to struggle anymore. They are along for the ride to observe the here and now. They may drift into the illusion from time to time but can quickly come out and step outside themselves as an uninterested observer. The more negative the experience the easier it is to see that they have fallen into the illusion. They easily empathize with those who are lost in the illusion. The enlightened ones can help the lost ones if they are willing to accept help, often they are not. Many do not want to face the possibility that their belief system is flawed. That is ok, because in the end of this life no matter what you believe, what will happen, will happen and your beliefs will not change that.

Do not expect perfect behavior from yourself or anyone who has realized their own enlightenment. You and they are still flawed characters in the illusion of life. There may still be losses of temper, hurtful words spoken, and other actions that upon reflection seem inappropriate or imperfect. This is the nature of beast. A self-aware person may be able recognize these thoughts and actions more quickly, and be able to diffuse the drama rapidly.

How about those rare saintly people like Mother Theresa? The soon to be Saint Blessed Theresa of Calcutta, was one of the most selfless persons to ever have graced this planet. The Catholic Church has begun the steps necessary to recognize her officially as a saint. She won a Nobel Peace Prize in 1979 for humanitarian work. There is also no doubt based on her diary that she had a complete crisis of faith for the last 50 years of her life. She believed there was nothing but blackness and cold in the afterlife. She mentioned that people saw her as forever smiling and not knowing how little faith she had. She even doubted the existence of God. If she had seen her true self, become aware of her enlightenment she may have not have suffered for the better part of her life.

Can a saintly person become enlightened? Yes they may, as much as you or any other person. They may have bigger obstacles to overcome than most within the illusion. Their egos are reinforcing the illusion upon them. It is difficult to fight the illusion head-on; it is easier to step around it.

Chapter 6

THE STATE OF ENLIGHTENMENT

There are a lot books including those covering non-duality that address the state of enlightenment. Many of these books do not talk about how to get there yourself, but to a certain extent spoon out enlightenment in small doses to keep you coming back for more. There is a Chinese proverb that says, "Give a man a fish and you feed him for a day. Teach a man to fish and you feed him for a lifetime." This proverb is custom made for those seeking enlightenment. Having said that, I also think it is helpful to have a greater understanding of some of the possibilities that may be expected as well as some of the misconceptions.

Everyone's experiences are unique when it comes to life in the illusion. Two people can be standing shoulder to shoulder and experience something in close proximity. They can each have different interpretation of the objective experience, what they saw, heard, and physically felt. They will have an even a greater degree of divergence on the subjective experience. One may experience horror and the other Nirvana. At the least, their subjective experience will be unique to each. One may interpret the experience negatively because it does not conform to their pre-conceived notion of their belief system, therefore it must be wrong or possibly evil. The other may perceive the experience as an awakening to a greater truth, because their belief system allows it as a possibility or they no longer require the filter of a belief system to interpret their reality.

The notion of unique experiences extends to a smaller degree to those who have become self-aware, and who no longer depend on belief systems to interpret reality. The self-aware person, when in a state of here-and-now absolute awareness, will observe experiences as a detached third person with minimal emotional attachment. However, depending upon their experiences and past beliefs their mind will capture and focus on a unique subjective subset of the overall experience.

Upon self-realization in rare cases, some may have extreme physical affectations as a change or enhancement in sensual awareness. They may see in more vivid colors, have more clarity of vision, see auras, etc. Their hearing may become more acute. More commonly, one may experience a greater appreciation for everything around them both large and small because of living in the present moment, the here and the now.

Chapter 7

METHODS OF MINDFULNESS

To become a spectator of one's own life is to escape the suffering of life.

Oscar Wilde

The Methods-of-Mindfulness are techniques to use during your settling-in period to help you adjust and accept your new realizations and the death of the facade. Your entire life you have been walking around asleep. Once awakened, these techniques will help you stay awake. You may have little use for these after a period of adjustment.

After the initial shock of self-realization settles in, the fun part can begin. Welcome to your new life as an enlightened being. Once you have become self-aware and understand the non-dual nature of reality you can revel in the playground of organic reality, otherwise known as the Maya.

There are no practices, disciplines, prayers, or techniques you have to engage in once you have become self-realized. There are several techniques that you may find helpful in maintaining your "buzz" that you have recently discovered. It does not matter in the end if you use these techniques or others or not. Once you realize your true self you can never deny it again. Whatever you believe is of no consequence either, because in the end reality is what it is, no matter what you hope it to be. No amount of faith, praying, meditation, or hoping will change the basic constructs of reality.

Stay With the I-Awareness
Be mindful of yourself as the I-Awareness. Realize that you are the awareness. You have all ready proved it to yourself. Keep out of your thoughts. You are not the contents of your thoughts you are that which is observing them. Let your mind do its thing and just observe it.

Meditation
The true purpose of meditation is to lose your mind. That is to forget about your mind and to quiet the mind so that you become the here and the now awareness. Do not meditate to achieve mystical experiences. These experiences will not bring about enlightenment recognition. During meditation for the purposes of gaining enlightenment, you may have mystical experiences, but this is not the goal and is not important if you have them or not.

You can meditate to quiet the mind and turn down the volume on the distractions of the illusion. There are many books and guides about meditation. This book will not go into great depth on any one method, other than to say that now you should limit your efforts to achieving awareness in the here and now. Quiet your mind to remove the noise so you can fully experience your awareness. Do not seek mystical experiences to achieve higher levels of enlightenment. There is only one level of enlightenment and you or either aware of it or you or not. Once you become aware of it, you cannot become aware of it at a higher level.

If you want to practice meditation for effects or experiences within the illusion, go for it, but remember the experiences are still only within the illusion.

The Monkey Mind

The Monkey Mind is what many of the eastern teachers refer to when they are talking about that nasty little creature that generates random thoughts in your mind. He is a chaotic creature and has a severe case of Attention-Deficit Hyperactivity Disorder (ADHD). He randomly bounces ideas around in your head that temporarily captures your awareness. As soon as you pay attention to one thought, he has an endless chain of them to feed you as fast as you can take them. The Monkey Mind is annoying if you are trying to still your mind and be in silence. People who are asleep in the waking dream are fully focusing on the monkey mind. They are too engaged to see that they are asleep and in a dream.

How do you deal with the Monkey Mind? You need to be as persistent as it is. When it sends you a thought, let it pass and go back to the silence. Do this over and over, and over again. Do not get mad at yourself for not being able to stop it. Celebrate yourself every time you recognize that a random thought is trying to steal your attention. You caught it in the act. Now let it pass. It is like a stubborn little child who will not stay in his seat. Whenever the child gets up, sit the child back down without emotion. It is a matter of automatic action-reaction, no emotion. Monkey Mind gives you thought (action), you let pass without emotion (reaction). Just like breathing; you inhale (action), you exhale (reaction). Listening to non-verbal music or tones can also be helpful as well. Do not listen to music with lyrics. The Monkey Mind loves the lyrics, as they give it catalysts for more thoughts to shove right back at your awareness. Mantras are also helpful in taming the Mind as well. Use a mantra such as "OHM" and repeat it in order to drown out the Monkey Mind from your focus. Focus on the Mantra for a while until the Monkey Mind is temporarily subdued.

Do not give the Monkey Mind more energy by wasting any time thinking or worrying about it, or for that matter, disliking or hating it. The Monkey Mind is like the scorpion, it is what is and it does what it does. Let it do its thing and you do yours. Live and let live. You need to focus on being the observer not the contents of your observation, for you are the Awareness, not the illusion.

Follow Your Breath

This is a common technique used with many disciplines. In its simplest form, breathe slowly in and out following your breath mentally as it comes into your body and fills your lungs. Follow the breath as it leaves your lungs and flows out of your body again. By doing this, you are observing your body breathing and you are not focusing on your thoughts, you are focusing on your breath and your body. You are in the present moment awareness as the observer. During this activity, you have retracted from your body/mind/ego and into your true essence of Awareness.

Third Person

Step outside yourself and watch your life being lived. Observe yourself interact with other illusory beings, as you would watch characters in a movie. Take a walk in nature and look at nature as an alien visitor to this planet. It is all new and fresh again. Take the third person point of view. Watch and do not participate. The illusion of you will do what it has to do. You do not need to worry about what your character needs to do, watch it live the life.

Mr. Robot

Take ride in Mr. Robot. Look at your hands. Move your fingers and observe the texture of your skin. Watch the smoothness of your movements. Realize that you are aware of your body, which is like a robot you are occupying. See how amazing it is. Know that is an artificial being that you are observing and experiencing life through. Close your eyes a do not move your hands. Feel the energy of their presence. Come to a non-conceptual understanding that they are there without having to move, touch or see them to confirm their aliveness.

Stop Thinking

Try to stop thinking. Try to stop thinking for five minutes. Unless you are an extremely accomplished meditator it will not happen. Your ego is on autopilot generating thought. It is not you. Your ego is not real. It is an illusion. When the thoughts do come up, notice that they are not of your choosing and they come from nowhere. You do not ever choose to be unhappy, but unhappy and sad thoughts come up all the time. Do not attach yourself to these thoughts. Examine them and let them go. These thoughts, any thoughts are not you. Life is being lived and you can observe it as a third person.

Chapter 8

AWAKEN IN NATURE

Nature: The Gates to Heaven

Nature has an irresistible allure to anyone who is even partially awake and a powerful magnetic pull to those in the process or fulfillment of awakening.

Growing up in a rural area in Southern Indiana, I had access to hundreds of acres of nature right outside my house. There were woods, meadows, streams, ponds, lakes, hills, valleys, and farmland all around me. If the weather was halfway decent, meaning it was not thunder storming or raining heavily, it was rare when I was not exploring nature for some part of my day. I would often leave my house with no particular plan, route or goal in mind and follow my instincts into the woods. If all else failed, I would follow a stream through the woods to see what was happening in the neighborhood of nature. It was never disappointing. There is always something exciting happening in nature right now.

Before I understood formal ideas and methods about observation in nature, I had several special spots that I would stop, sit and observe nature. Some of the spots I knew had particular animals that lived or frequented, like foxes, groundhogs, chipmunks, squirrels, birds, amphibians, and fish. Whatever I experienced at these spots or on my nature walks was always thrilling. I used to think this was the greatest show on earth and nothing else came close. It seems to be a million times greater than before with my new Awareness.

What I later came to understand is that nature is a lot more than what meets the senses. It is a highly concentrated focal point of energy awareness. It is the world of the non-ego. Ego has no audience to impress or receive rounds of adulation from; the other egos are not around. It is the easiest place to see that you are not the contents of your thoughts and that you are the awareness. The inhabitants of the world of nature, the rocks, the animals, the plants, fire, water, and air are all living their existence in the here and now, in presence awareness. This even applies to our domestic plants and animals. Animals do not think about what they are going to have for dinner later in the day, they are fully focused and aware of what is happening right now. Experience the stoic stillness of a tree or a rock.

The ego has little support and validation in nature. Human interaction and the non-natural world is where ego is at its strongest. The non-natural world is also the place where it is much more difficult to avoid thoughts and memories. This world is constantly challenging your ego to validate and defend itself by others and the physical reality that surrounds it. Thoughts are the world of ego. Nature is the world of the One.

Nature Awareness

For many years, I taught classes on animal tracking, and advanced awareness and movement in nature. At the time, I did not realize that what I was teaching was Awareness in the here and the now within in the illusion of nature. I had incredible experiences while using these techniques. Now these same techniques result in a magnification of Awareness and experience unimaginable in my recent past, because I am now self-aware and non-conceptually understand that the Maya is an illusion and there is only the One.

You can view and experience everything now as though you are an alien from different dimension far away. It is all new, fresh, and detailed in infinite layers of complexity, elegance, and beauty. It is amazing and rapturous. You can explore your new world in many ways, but here are a few ideas that may give you a jump-start.

Look at the Small to See the Big

While teaching animal tracking class or even while practicing your own tracking skills, you must first learn to see at different levels of magnification. This may or may not require optical enhancement like magnifying glasses or reading glasses according to the acuity of your eyesight. The most important things happen beyond the actual seeing and more at the level of recognition and awareness of what you are seeing.

When many people think of animal tracking, they think of clear mud track identification. Track identification is one of the ten arts of tracking which we will not explore in this text. A lot of what tracking is about is exploring in detail everything around the tracks, away from the tracks and in the tracks with all five senses, while integrating the five senses along with intuition into a sixth sense. In other words, real animal tracking involves intense awareness.

I tell my tracking students when you look into an animal track you need to lie down on the ground get your face right up close to the track and see every detail of the impressions made in the track. I tell them to view each grain of sand as if it were a six-foot tall boulder. Look at the boulders in relationship to one another and the patterns left by pressures exerted by the feet that left these tracks. I tell them to draw every detail in a track, which may take a few hours to accomplish. I tell them to study the track and the drawing in relationship to the other tracks around it and to explore everything around the tracks with all six senses. They must learn to understand the Oneness of everything around the tracks and themselves. They must learn to conduct an inquiry into what they have observed, such as what are these plants right here next to the track, what are the plants three feet away, why did the animal go around the shrub to the right and not the left. One can ask an infinite amount of questions, and the more answers you find to the minute questions, the more you understand the big picture.

This type of animal tracking where you go into the field lie on the ground and spend hours studying a few tracks is called dirt time and it is invaluable in understanding nature to a greater degree.

You may be asking at this point, "What does this have to do with Living in the Here and the Now?" I know of no greater way of experiencing the here and the now than with intimate immersion with nature. This will take you and your mind far away from the stickiest and densest aspects of the emotionally charged experience of the Maya in close proximity to others. It is just you and the awesome beauty of the spectacle of nature. You may begin to experience nature with a completely different perspective while simultaneously focusing your Awareness in the here and the now.

You do not have to be well versed in the skills of tracking to benefit greatly from this activity. Go outside and find an animal track. You may not need to go far from your house to do this. You can also look at the tracks of domestic or wild animals or even humans. It does not matter. The idea is to immerse yourself in the details of the tracks and the nature around you.

Look at the track in detail, look at the ridges and impressions in the track, and ask yourself questions. Look at the plants, insects, rocks, and debris around the tracks. Listen to the birds singing. When you hear the bird singing, really listen. Try to spot and identify the bird. Does this bird's presence have anything to do with this track or the animal that made it? Look at how beautiful the bird is. Listen to the joy in the song it sings. Does the bird have a mate or a nest nearby?

Look at spatial relationships between the individual tracks the plants, and manmade structures. Does this spatial relationship answer any questions about the who, where, what, when, how, and why of this track? Who made this track, where was this animal going and coming from? When was this track made? Why was one part of the track deeper the rest? Look at the next track, see the sand boulders, look at their beauty, and ask more questions. Do this for a while and pause to think about how much more detail, elegance, beauty, and complexity is in this small area of nature that you did not even know existed a few hours ago.

This is an infinitely small snapshot of what is going in the here and the now within the illusion of Maya on this tiny planet we call earth. Earth as you recall is like a subatomic particle in this universe and you have superficially explored a very insignificantly small part of it. You have not even scratched the surface of how deep you can go. Marvel in that.

Another World in Organic Reality

This idea comes from another technique I used when teaching advanced awareness in nature. In the classroom, I taught methods of walking and moving in nature that slowed the pace, gave incredible balance and control, and reduced the noise of walking in nature. These techniques allowed the students to blend into nature and become a part of nature in ways they were previously not aware. The advantage to this is that the animals in nature will not flee in terror from the encroachment of the awkward, scary presence of a large viscous predator entering their world.

After teaching them the basic movement techniques, I would take the class outside in a wooded area and blindfold them. Some distance away I would play some Native American music and have them walk toward the music with quiet confidence with their newly discovered abilities. The learning experience of this blindfold walking is twofold. First, it was to help each individual to learn not to rely solely on his or her vision for moving safely and quietly across the landscape. It also teaches us how to rely more on our other five senses, including the sixth. Secondly and more importantly, for the purposes of experiencing the here and the now, it transports you into a different awareness of organic reality. Maybe for the first time in your life you feel the subtle breeze upon your cheek, the reflection of heat from a nearby tree, or the sensation from your mind's eye of the aura of a plant or person nearby.

From this viewpoint, organic reality feels and looks different. You become aware of aspects of your world that you overlooked with your eyes open. Smell the pine pitch from the tree three feet away from you at a forty-five degree angle on your right. Hear the fly buzz over your head. Feel the vibrations of the energy of life all around you. Sense the subtle differences in its ebbs and flows. Hear your own breathing. Feel and hear your heartbeat. This is not the everyday reality for which you are accustomed.

The reactions I received from my students from this exercise were amazing. They were always thrilled beyond description when they completed the exercise as if they had come back from a short visit from some exotic land, which they had.

I emphasized to my students before this exercise to pay particular attention to your intuition, your physical feelings of tension and lightness in their body that represented positive and negative information. After one class, a man in his upper fifties approached me with tears in eyes and told me that, what he experienced in this exercise was the same thing he experienced while in the jungles of Vietnam. He said that he learned to listen to his inner voice of intuition and it saved his life many times. He was not able to explain it to anyone and no one understood it. This was the first time that he was able to reconnect with that part of himself and was grateful for helping him understand what was going on. Of course, I did not teach him anything, I showed him where to look.

Since it is difficult for you to learn the technique of self-confident blindfolded walking from a book, you can still derive a majority of the benefits of this exercise by doing it on your hands and knees by crawling very slowly while blindfolded. Even while doing the blindfolded walk; the goal is to move at sixty six seconds per step or less. Your movement on your hands and knees you should be no faster. Stop as often and as long as you like. Your goal is not to go anywhere. You are already there. The movement facilitates a new perspective on the here and the now from a slightly different vantage point.

Tap Into Your Sixth Sense

The ultimate goal here is to tap into your sixth sense and to fully embrace the here and the now.

The Secret Spot

The Secret Spot is another technique that I used in the advance awareness and movement class. Perform this technique in a solitary setting. Practice this technique daily, at least for the purposes of nature awareness, over a period of about a year or more. Use this technique to become intimately familiar with a solitary spot in nature, much as you are with your body. Likewise you can also use this technique to experience the here and the now and presence awareness to its fullest.

Find a place in nature that you are able to visit frequently and easily. It can be in your back yard or on your patio. Anywhere you are able to observe nature up close and personal. When using this for the purposes of Nature awareness you must stagger the times of day, weather conditions, and any other variables that may have an effect on your secret spot. For the purpose of Awareness Presence that will not be necessary. If you desire, you may place a chair or a cushion at your secret spot for more comfort.

This technique is about awareness and place. You will use all the techniques found in the two previous exercises of animal tracking and Awareness in Nature, but they will always been done at your secret spot. You will also do more than this as well. You will know things about your secret spot that nobody else ever will know unless you tell them. While at your Secret Spot, you will conduct inquiries into everything you observe with your six senses.

On the first day at your secret spot, bring a notebook. The first thing you need to do is draw a picture of everything you see in as much detail as possible. Do not worry if your sketching skills are marginal. This sketch is for you to develop a mental map of your Secret Spot. Include all buildings, trees, contours of terrain; water etc. in your sketch. Determine which way is North and mark it on your drawing. Fill in some of the major areas of vegetation, capturing its relative height as compared to other vegetation around it. Make it good enough that you understand everything you put into the sketch. After your sketch is complete, you can use it over time to fill in more details after your visits with your secret spot. The goal of the first visit is to get an overview of the topographic and the initial introduction to your secret spot.

On subsequent visits, you must write in your notebook or journal, the time, the date, and the weather conditions, where the sun and the moon are in the sky relative to your position. You must stay at least twenty minutes to give nature a chance to settle back down to their base level after your intrusion. If you choose to vary the time of day, you will see dramatic differences.

Observe everything around you using the techniques described in tracking and nature awareness. This observation includes the birds that you see and hear, the other sounds you hear, the feeling of the wind and sun on your skin and hair, the heat or cold in the area, your emotional impressions, etc. Look at the animal tracks in your Secret Spot and do the inquiries. Were these tracks there yesterday? What is the who, where, what, how, when, and why of these tracks. What are those small plants near your feet? Are they edible or medicinal, if so, how? Do these plants have any other uses for humans or nature? You may need to access reference materials such as plant guides, insect and animal guides after each encounter. Observe how the animals and insects behave. Does the current weather or time of year, time of day have any effect upon them? How does your presence or the presence of other animals affect them? Observe every minute detail and ask yourself questions about their meaning. Use every tool at your disposal.

Avoid Labeling

Some labeling and identification may be necessary at first. Let go of that as soon as possible. The natural tendency of the mind upon recognizing something is to identify it, label it and move on. To say that if you indentify a cricket, a bunch of grass, some trees, and hear a few birds, you have experienced nature in the present moment totally misses the mark. You have only begun the process of becoming aware of something in nature and only at a superficial level.

The initial recognition is nothing more than a cue to an opportunity to experience the here and the now. As far as the mind is concerned, once you label something, the mind has completed its job for that instance and it will move on. If you see a movement in your lawn out of the corner of your eye, look in that direction and recognize that the movement is a Robin. The brain is finished; it has done its job, and flitters to the next object or the next random thought. This is the Monkey Mind in action. As the content of your awareness is not your awareness.

A label is not the thing it identifies. A label is a label. The name you associate with on an object is not the object itself; it is no more than a label. Labeling gives power to the illusion and takes you out of the here and the now. Dismiss the labels in your mind as soon as possible and go directly to Awareness of the essence of what you are experiencing, right here, right now. Have no tolerance of thoughts of the past or the future. Do not think about what you will be having for lunch, who you will be seeing later etc. Be in the here and the now.

The purpose of the secret spot is to become one with your Secret Spot and everything within it. It is to gain the sixth sense awareness of this extension of yourself, to feel the aliveness and energy of the place and its inhabitants. That is to say to extent the concept of yourself beyond your body. As you can feel the aliveness in various parts of your body and know it is there without moving it, seeing it or touching it, you can do the same in nature beyond your body. It is all one.

The Secret Spot in a New Light
Visit your Secret Spot with a blindfold on and make observations of you experience without the assistance of your vision. You will experience it differently than you do when your vision is not impaired. Try using a blindfold and ear muffs. Shut off two senses. You will still observe amazing things in the here and the now. Go to your Secret Spot in night and day and during the changes of the guard at dawn and dusk. These are the times when the diurnal and nocturnal life forms come on or go off the nature scene. Very few things are as exciting as waiting in the dark for the sun to rise and hearing the first daylight song birds sing with magnificent joy celebrating the arrival of the sun. They will start about twenty or thirty minutes before light in some cases, so do not be late for the show. It is amazing!

During this process, become absorbed with your awareness of your observations, not the content of your awareness. The content of your awareness is the illusion. The illusion is amazing, beautiful and elegant; but your awareness and ability to be fully in the here and the now of this illusion is the real crown jewel. You are observing through the instrument of your illusory self, using your body/mind/ego as a tool to observe and be aware of the Maya. You are Pure Awareness.

Repeat this exercise as often as possible, and if the mood hits you take some time to meditate upon what your Awareness is doing and the implications of this upon your understanding of reality. This will help you stay focused in the here and the now in your day-to-day experience of organic reality.

Visit with a Tree

I have always loved trees. My earliest memories of my close association with a tree was when I was a boy growing up in a quite neighbor in town. Several Black Locust trees saplings sprouted at the edge of our property line. I was attracted to those trees and one in particular I decided to adopt as my own. I remember visiting that tree during the entire 10 years I lived there. On many occasions, I would talk to the tree and would listen in silence. It never spoke back to me, but I felt at the time that it did appreciate my attention as I appreciated the tree.

Nowadays I still visit with individual trees. Mostly I do not speak at all; I listen. I listen with my intuition; I listen to its silence. I join with the tree's Isness, its sense of aliveness and awareness. A tree is patient and a tree is quiet. Listen and learn from the trees.

Visit with a Flower

A flower is a fleeting expression of the energy and Oneness of the universe. A flower is delicate and an expression of joy in the here and the now. It is the metaphor for awakening. Flowers show us what it is like to be fully awake and present. Visit with flowers and be with them in the silence of the here and the now.

Find a flower either outdoors or in your own home. Sit by the flower and quiet your mind. You may want to do a short meditation to get yourself in the grove. Look at the flower and enjoy the beauty and the positive energy that it radiates. If the Monkey Mind visits while you are with the flower, deal with it as described previously. It wants your attention always. This is your time to be with the flower.

Grasshopper

I have always been attracted to grasshoppers. They are elegant and perfectly engineered miracles of nature. You may have the same attraction for ants or other insects. Spend some time with these amazing creatures. Look at their beauty and the perfection of their movement. With all the technology we have on earth today, nothing comes close to the sophistication and the miracle of these insects. They have awareness and are living in the present moment. They carry out their entire life cycle in perfect presence awareness. Be with your insect friends and learn from their silence. Listen with your intuition and see what they have to teach.

The World of the Crystal

Relate to crystals in much the same way as described with insects. They do not move and they do not die, at least during our lifetime and they are ancient, millions of years old. You can feel their energetic vibration, if you quiet your mind and listen with your intuition.

Nature at Night

Nature at night is thrilling. A new cast of characters comes out at night to live their lives. There are many birds including owls, nighthawks, nightjars, and others. The amphibians are at their pick activity at night. Many of the mammals in North America are primarily nocturnal, using the cover of darkness to hide their presence. The mammal predators are out at night hunting those who are using the darkness for cover. This is a type of time-sharing within nature where daytime niches of one species share the space with different nighttime species.

Go out at night to a natural spot. Sit and listen with your ears and your intuition. Feel the buzz of the energy of the nighttime. Feel its aliveness. You may hear some scary noises that you have never heard before. In many cases they are some of the birds, insects, amphibians, and mammals you may have never seen or even knew existed in your area. Be present with the nighttime in nature. It is truly wonderful.

Your Own Awareness Encounters

You can also create your own personal exercises and activities to further focus and enhance your awareness of the here and the now. It can all only happen in the present moment, so do not look at some prolonged discipline to get you some promised experience in the distant future. Remember it is not about the content of the awareness, your experience, that is important or real, it is about your awareness that is happening right here, right now. There is always something awesome happening in the here and the now. Do not miss it. It is all here for you.

Chapter 9

MORE POINTERS

Jesus said, "I stood at rest in the midst of the world. And unto them I was shown forth incarnate; I found them all intoxicated. And I found none of them thirsty. And my soul was pained for the children of humankind, for they are blind in their hearts and cannot see. For, empty did they enter the world, and again empty they seek to leave the world. But now they are intoxicated. When they shake off their wine then they will have a change of heart."

Gospel of Saint Thomas

The preceding four totalities show you something you need to investigate. They point you in the right direction for you to find the non-conceptual knowingness. They are concepts used to gain non-conceptual understanding and it is something only you can learn for yourself. No one can really teach you any of this. Parroting back the words of a concept you have learned is only an intellectual understanding. This will not get you to self-realization. Intellectual understanding will not get you to the end of your search. It will only give you some interesting information that you may or may not choose to believe. You will only need these pointers temporarily while getting the non-conceptual realization to settle.

I grew up in the hill country of Southern Indiana and went to college at Purdue in the northern plains of Indiana. During a hunting trip that I will never forget, a local student, my roommate, and I went deer hunting. This was in an area the local student had hunted many times before. He told us to go toward a stand of trees and wait on the hill near the creek where he would rendezvous with us. My roommate and I walked toward the creek and could not find the hill. After a while, we walked back to the truck where our northern friend was still getting ready and told him that we did not see a hill near the creek.

We argued for a while and he pointed and said, "It is right over there, don't you see it?" We answered, "No we do not. There is no hill over there." Frustrated, he walked us to the creek and stopped. He pointed straight down and said, "We are standing on the hill." Much to our amazement the hill was about a two-foot swell in the ground, that to our hill country eyes, did not even register as anything but flat ground. We thought the ground was flat. We realized that the ground in Northern Indiana really is not flat. From that point on, we could see the hills in northern Indiana and we never doubted it again. We had gained a non-conceptual understanding of the non-flatness of Northern Indiana. It was all in knowing where and how to look. Here are some more pointers:

Be like a Child

And said, Verily I say unto you, Except ye be converted, and become as little children, ye shall not enter into the kingdom of heaven.

Matthew 18:3

Look at the youngest of children and notice how everything is fresh, new, and exciting. They have no sense of a separate identity. They are just in the present moment, not thinking of the past or the future, just the here and the now. They are not labeling, judging or identifying anyone or anything, even themselves. They do not think about their relationships, their careers, their to-do lists. They are not aware of their bodies, their minds, or their egos. They will later learn all of these things including identifying themselves as a separate person.

This is a case of less is more. The less you label, think, identify, or remember, the more you will be in the here and the now. The more you are in the here in the now the more you will experience unconditional bliss and happiness. When you are like a child you are not experiencing separateness. You are experiencing the "isness" of being. You are just "Awareness."

This begs the question of what is the difference between an enlightened adult and an infant. As the scripture says, "you must become as little children before you can enter the kingdom of heaven." The attributes of infants described above are the same attributes you must strive to obtain to realize your enlightenment. The difference is that an enlightened adult has all the facilities of understanding and knowledge of self as ego and is still able to see their enlightenment. Infants have yet to overcome these impediments and have not immersed themselves in the dream, but are only observing the dream. Enlightened adults must learn how to observe the dream while still participating in it.

Achievement of Happiness

You cannot do anything to achieve happiness. Achievement of happiness occurs in the Non-Conceptual here and now of Self-illuminated Presence Awareness. When you forget about your mind and thoughts and are just with your awareness in the here and now, the Presence Awareness, you experience true happiness. Think back on your happiest moments. During those periods, you were not thinking about yourself, just the experience. Even if that experience was happening through your physical body, you were not thinking of your body, your mind or your ego. You were just "Awareness."

Your mind and your thoughts are your ego. Ego attempts to make sense of your life. It will try to bring your unconscious thoughts together with your conscious thoughts, when in reality it cannot do it! Let your ego go. Your ego will try to burden you with all of its imaginary problems. The ego and all its delusional issues are fantasy. They are not real. They will eventually die, as unlike your true self, they have no permanence. The true you of your ever-present awareness will never die. You can only find happiness in the here and now.

Know Intellectually

If you say that you understand your non-duality intellectually, just drop the word intellectually. If you have done the self-inquiry and have seen your true self, then you know it non-conceptually. You either know it or you do not. The word intellectually is a crutch the ego uses. It is trying to convince you that you cannot achieve this, because if you do, the ego will be invalidated. Do not let your ego take possessions of your awareness.

Investigate Life's Issues

When something comes up in your life that is causing you attachment, sorrow, anger, hurt, or pain, investigate it. Perform some self-inquiry. Ask yourself, "Who is the doer? Who is the object of the doing? Are any of the characters including you real? Is any of this real anyway?"

Be Without Labeling

Look around and do not label or catalog, just be the Awareness. That is all you truly are. Do not think about yourself, your body, your mind, your ego, your issues, or your problems. Do not identify yourself.

There is always something fascinating happening right here right now. Look around, it is all ever fresh, ever new, and endlessly fascinating. The illusion is magnificent. Enjoy it!

Pain

Pain does not happen to you. It happens to your body, which is not you. It is extremely demanding, but do not forget it is just another experience. Just be with it, like any other experience. This one may take some effort because the illusion is powerful. Remember and be aware of what you truly are.

Fear of Loss of Memory

There is a great fear of losing one's memory, because the ego identifies itself with memory. It turns out that memory is not reliable. The accuracy of what you actually remember is low and your mind just fills in the rest, so it seems that you remember everything. The fear is that if you lose your memory, you will lose yourself. You would be happier if you did. Memories are just thoughts of what your brain has assimilated as its estimation of past events. Nothing happens in the past, only in the present.

Forgive Yourself

You may have had failures and made mistakes in your past that you regret. These memories cause you pain. You feel guilty about them. You wish you could do them over. You may feel that you are somehow flawed or do not have a place in this world, the odd man out. Great news, you, the real you is perfect. You or no one else needs to forgive you. The you that made those mistakes is not real. This you that made those mistakes did not have a choice anyway as it has no free will. It is just playing a part and is driven by deterministic cause and effect.

Past events and memories never happened. You never hurt anyone or yourself. You are worrying about a fictional character, a character in your dream. These statements are not platitudes to convince you that you are ok. The you that made the mistakes is a fairy tale. It is not you. Get over yourself. You as a separate entity do not exist.

Lose Your Ego

To the degree that you can lose or suppress your ego the greater amount of happiness you will have. Totally losing your ego will give you total unending happiness. The ego or mind takes ownership of thoughts, memories, and emotions after they have spontaneously arrived. In doing this the ego validates its existence by saying that these all came from me(ego), when in fact they did not. Do not try to destroy the ego you will only make it stronger by giving it attention. The diminishment and destruction of the ego will happen as a side effect of understanding that you do not exist. Forget yourself and you will find yourself. All suffering comes from the idea that you are a separate identity or ego. Lose yourself and find paradise.

Happiness is in the Here and the Now

You can only be happy now. You can only be anything in the here and now. There is no future or past, only present. Do not wait, put-off, or plan for some future happiness. Happiness can only happen in the now. Be now. Remember, time is an illusion. What are you waiting for be happy now.

Test for Realness and the Illusion

A good test to see if something is real is to ask if it changes. If it is real then it will not change. It will remain constant.

Lewis and Clark documented the state of the Ohio River during their expedition. They spoke of fish so large and numerous in the Ohio River that you could almost walk across their backs. Do you think the Ohio River of 200 years ago is the same as the one today? This clearly illustrates the changing nature of the unreal or the illusion.

Shed Your Outer Layers
Shed and dismiss all the outer layers of ego, body, brain, and mind. These prevent you from seeing what you already are and where you want to be. What is left is what you already are.

Discard what is not real to reveal what is real, like the great sculptors who report that all they do is remove all the rock that does not belong to reveal the magnificent sculpture that was already in the rock.

You Do Not Have to Do Anything
There are no techniques, practices, meditation, worshipping, or praying necessary to become enlightened. You have always been and always will be enlightened. You do not need to do any of these things to recognize your enlightenment either. Conduct the self-inquiry and the truth will set you free.

You Never Did Anything
There is not a you that ever existed to do anything. Nobody who ever lived ever existed or ever did anything, no more than a fictional character in a book or a movie. The reality that your ego desperately clings to does not exist. It is like a dream and once you wake up, you will see it is only a dream.

Lucid Wakefulness
In your illusion of life, you sometimes have lucid dreams, where you wake up in the dream and know you are dreaming. Now, you are going to have a lucid wakefulness where you cannot fall permanently back sleep. The dream you are becoming lucid in, is the organic life you used to think was reality. You may have moments where you fall back to sleep in this organic reality, but unlike in a sleeping dream anything

that excites you negatively or positively will remind you that it is just a dream. If you have any uncertainty, take a peek, do the self-inquiry and reconfirm what you non-conceptually know.

Suffering Never Totally Goes Away
Suffering will never totally go away. There is no permanent escape from the vicissitudes of everyday living, as long as you are participating in or observing the illusion. Suffering can be greatly reduced or its duration diminished by reconfirming your understanding and becoming an observer to the suffering all the while realizing that there is no you that is suffering. The true you cannot be burned by fire, cut by a sword or hurt in anyway. It is immutable.

Know You Do Not Exist 24/7
Know there is no you 24/7, just as you know the sun will return after cloud passes. You do not need to think about this 24/7, just as you do not have to think about the sun's existence continuously. Reconfirm until you know it constantly and it is second nature. Your Goal is to unconditional understand your true nature 24/7.

Belief Causes Suffering
Belief that you are a person, an individual identity is the cause of all your suffering. Come to know without reservation what you truly are. If you non-conceptually know something is true then belief is not necessary. You know there is no separate self and you cannot be harmed.

Want Nothing
Want and desire nothing. Want and desire are characteristics of the ego. Wants and desires are a hoping for something in the future. There is no future, only the here and now. The future is just a thought that appears in your mind. It is not real and you have no control over it. Understanding that wants and desires are unreal thoughts will allow you to

observe them and let them pass. Being with the here and the now are of your true self. Just be now, you do not have to wait for happiness!

It May Take Some Time

You have been living with the concept that you are a separate and real person for your whole life. It may take some time to replace that belief with the new realization that you are the One. Give it some time to settle in and stabilize. You will probably have to revalidate your new reality several times before it fully settles. Keep rechecking to make sure and soon you will not need to check anymore.

You Have Been Taught Nothing

You have arrived at where you always were and I have taught you nothing. You have recognized what you truly are and always have been. You now have a heightened awareness of your true self and of the nature of organic and actual reality.

Shift from Contents of Awareness to the Awareness Itself

Shift your focus from the content of awareness, to awareness itself. The content of your awareness is what you experience, what you see, hear, taste, etc. The awareness itself is that which is being aware, that which is beyond your physical body and mind. You are the One and the One is all there is. The One is the Nothingness and Everything. You are the Everything and the Nothing (No-thing).

Look for the Seer

Look for the "me" that is doing the seeing and the "thinker" who is doing the thinking. You will not find them. When your body dies, do your eyes still see? No they do not, so your body was not doing the seeing. Will you still be aware? Yes, you will.

Do Not Fall into the Trap

Do not fall into the trap of thinking that you are enlightened. The "I" and the "me" are the ego. Do not declare anything; the ego will take ownership of anything you declare. Just be the Awareness. Just be the Enlightenment. The ego does not need to be included because it is only by leaving the ego behind that the awareness can be realized. The Awareness defies attempts to capture it with conceptual thought. It is non-conceptual. Do not declare; just be!

Meditate without Expectation

If you are seeking enlightenment, do not meditate to have mystical experiences. Mystical experiences are not enlightenment; they are experiences in the illusion of organic reality. You do not need to meditate or do anything else to become enlightened, wake-up, become aware, or get it. It requires no work, only recognition that the body, brain, mind, and ego do not exist and they never have. You can meditate to be in the here and now and become the awareness.

There is Nothing to Achieve

There is nothing to achieve, nothing to brag about, no challenge to overcome, nothing to be accomplished. You are already enlightened and perfect. The ego needs and desires accomplishments so it can declare some victory or achievement. Do not feel sad for your ego. It will just have to get over itself; sorry ego.

Judge Not

Judge not. Ego judges, sorts, and separates all. Awareness has no judgment, just unconditional acceptance, embracing all. Judge not and you shall not be judged.

You Can Go No Deeper

There is no need to go deeper than deep. Enlightenment recognition does not occur in levels. There are no levels of Enlightenment or Awareness. There are degrees of

Awakeness. Either you recognize your enlightenment or you do not.

Do Not Grieve the Death of Ego

If you get depressed or sad about the idea that your ego is not real, and it will not survive death, get over it. Remember, the root of all your suffering is your ego and it is never ending quest to validate its own existence. Your ego will never totally die while your body is still alive although with certain health conditions like coma or dementia it may be greatly subdued. You can always allow your ego to come out and play whenever you choose, but it no longer needs to be your master. Your ego is not permanent and it will not survive death

Chapter 10

WHAT NOW

Jesus said, "Let one who seeks not stop seeking until that person finds; and upon finding, the person will be disturbed; and being disturbed, will be astounded; and will reign over the entirety."

Gospel of Saint Thomas(2)

There is an old Zen saying that partially describes the post-recognition experience, "Before enlightenment, chop wood, carry water, after enlightenment, chop wood, carry water." This is a generalization, but life will go on as you know it in many ways. You will still sleep, wake-up, eat, breath, and so forth.

Do not anticipate a state of eternal bliss or euphoria, at least not while in the awareness of the illusion. You will probably not be walking on water or multiplying fishes and loaves, unless that is what the illusory-you is going to do. Life will still have highs and lows, but there will be significant differences as well.

Life will take on a simple easy grace. Your new motto for life may become, "Don't worry be happy." Previously you may have wondered if you would ever find true happiness and an ease with the world around you. As long as you do not focus on the illusion, you will find this type of happiness. Those who previously appeared to have it made, may now seem not as fortunate after all. Their happiness may seem a facade or fleeting at best. You now have the real deal and if you have friends or relatives who are truly searching, pass it on.

Some do not really want the suffering to end or are afraid not to believe the reality and perception of the afterlife and God they have come to understand. You can do nothing for those who are not ready. Not to worry, because in the end they will be ok as well, regardless of what they believe. They will not reap punishment or hold themselves back because they did not advance their understanding. They will experience a more difficult road while in this is illusion, but only within the illusion.

You will experience a great reduction in the seriousness of life as well. Issues will still come and go, and because you realize it is happening in the illusion, you will not be as concerned as you would have been otherwise. Situations that you previously would have considered extremely serious may now evoke laughter, as you know it is only happening within the illusion and is not real. Be cautious about expressing yourself too openly. Some may not be able to appreciate your new freedom and sense of humor. They may think you have lost your mind or that you have become callous and non-caring. Nothing could be further from the truth, as now you know you need not worry about any individual entity.

You can love all equally because there is only the One to love. You can release all worry, stress, guilt, and regret. You are free of all these burdens now that you realize your true nature. The lows will not be as low, but the highs will be much higher. Do not restrain your joy, it is ok to be happy as much as you like now.

There will be certain positive aspects of this new recognition that may resonate with you, such as the shedding of guilt and disgust for past actions or experiences. You can now forgive yourself and surrender. The burdens will dissolve, because you non conceptually know that the person you have previously identified as yourself is not real.

Whatever was bringing you the most anxiety in the past may attract most of your attention now, because the vacuum of suffering and anxiety left behind is now hard to ignore. It will take some to time to adjust to the idea of the end of this suffering. You may have to go back and revalidate that you actually understand your true nature and that this sea change in perspective has happened to you. Give it time and your attention with these issues will fade.

You still see, hear, feel, smell and touch as always. You now know the apparent separateness is an illusion. What is the difference now? Nothing and everything is different. Attachment, fear and suffering are gone. You become the observer.

> Nature is not hostile, nor yet is it friendly, it is simply indifferent.
>
> John Hughes Holmes

This quote applies to life as well. This is why bad things happen to good people. Innocent children die every day of starvation and abuse around the world. Good people are hurt, tortured, raped, and killed every day. You may ask, "How God could let these things happen?" Let us suppose that if it was not all an illusion maybe God would not let it happen, but it is an illusion so it will continue to happen. It is all make believe, all a dream and no one is really getting hurt.

Life will happen and you will witness it as a third person observer. It will be painful, happy, sad, mad, and glad. When you step back to the third person perspective of the Awareness, you will know it is all an illusion. It is what it is.

After a painful episode you may say, "That was fun. What is next? Bring it on!"

You do not need to change your name from something western sounding such as "Sailor" Bob Adamson to Sri Marahaba Swami. If your name was "Sailor" Bob Adamson before, then that label will work just as well afterwards. It is a label for an imaginary entity. Changing the label of Sailor Bob to Sri Marahaba Swami is similar to changing the name of a fictional character in novel. It may help the novel a little but it will not help the character. In ether event, these characters in organic reality do not exist. A tomato is a tomato. Changing its' name to orange will not make it an orange.

Even if you previously thought the organic reality was real, does not diminish the mystery and complexity of the natural or manmade world. Go for a walk, watch people, and revel in nature. Something amazing is always going on in the here and the now, just take a look. It is even more amazing when you understand the true nature of organic reality.

Strangely enough, successes in life seem to come more frequently and with greater ease. What you once struggled for and against seem to fall in your lap as soon as you give up the struggle. Since you now understand that it is all an illusion, you need not worry about outcomes and this puts you at an extreme advantage. Things will start to go your way. You will not have any say in how they go, because you have no free will. Nonetheless, more often than not a favorable outcome will occur that is better than you may have anticipated.

What is my Purpose in Life

Your primary purpose in life is the same as everyone else's primary purpose, because there is only the One. That purpose is to be awake in the here and now and to be aware of your enlightenment. In other words, stay awake in the here and now and observe your life being lived. As you begin to awaken and stay awake, you will find your secondary and unique purpose in life. Upon living in the here and the now your secondary purpose in life will align itself with your primary purpose.

Your secondary purpose in life will not come from figuring it out, but rather will come from the stillness within. You will need to keep alert to see the opportunities present themselves, because they will. When you become detached from the outcome, your organic life will begin to work itself out with amazing ease. Your secondary purpose will come naturally within your life without a struggle. There are not any coincidences, stay awake, stay alert, and stay in the here and now.

Some of the Beacons of Light

You have everything you need to point you to the truth right now. It is a matter of looking within and doing the self-inquiry. Once you get it, you will find that reading more Advaitan material becomes somewhat tedious as they are saying the same things and it is not anything you do not all ready understand. The difference is that you now non-conceptually understand ideas that previously looked contradictory or even nonsensical. They will now make perfect sense and you will quickly become bored with reading Advaita material, as you would quickly tire of reading about the earth being round and not flat. They are all really saying the same things from different perspectives. If you do feel you need additional reading or instruction on Advaiti, I have listed some of the more influential modern teachers. This is not an exhaustive list, there are many more, but here are some that I found to be lucid:

"Sailor" Bob Adamson
Sri Nisargadatta Maharaj
U.G. Krishnamurti
James Braha
Stephen Dewitt
Cameron Riley

Nathan Gill
Alan Watts
John Wheeler
Leo Hartong
Ekhart Tolle
Adyashanti

Chapter 11

CONCEPTUAL CONCERNS

But What about...

Whenever a "but what about" concern comes to mind, investigate who is asking by going back to the "Look for the Me." and conduct a self-inquiry. You will see that the concerns are coming from a conceptual self that does not exist. Therefore, the question is not important. If a character in your dream asks you a question, would you be concerned if that fictional character received a response the next night when you slept? Probably not, because that character is not real.

Who is doing the asking?

This is the answer you can use for all "but what about" concerns. This may not always satisfy your curiosity if your self-realization is recent. Eventually this universal Advaitan answer in the form of a question will satisfy you, but probably not at first.

Even though the concept of you being your mind-body-ego is totally an illusion, it seems incomplete somehow if we do not understand a few key concepts. None of these concerns really matter, because they are all about conceptual reality. I too initially sought answers that are more satisfying after I had my revelation. Most who are new to these ideas also share some common questions in order to feel complete and in their search.

I Cannot Get It

You are conceptualizing too much. Drop that concept and go look for "the me" right now. You will not find it. It is not there and there is no logic to suggest that it is. The only thing sustaining the belief that there is a separate identity is your ego. Your ego is fictional and it wants you to believe it is real. The ego's prime directive is to validate its' existence. Let go of the idea of the separateness and you will get it.

I had it and then I lost it

You cannot lose it, once you get it. Your ego has temporarily confused you. It has convinced you that it is real. It has convinced you emotionally and not logically. It is a lie. Go look for the reality of the ego. You will not find it. It is not real. Shed what is not real and what is left is the true you.

I Still Have Anxiety and Fear

I still have anxiety, guilt, and fear. I do not like these experiences. Who does not like these experiences? These experiences are like others, just thoughts. The experience of joy, happiness, sadness and anxiety are all experiences. What is the anxiety, a thought, a label? Where in your body is this anxiety happening?

All suffering comes from the idea that you, your ego is real. Your ego is not real. See where the suffering is happening. It is happening in your mind and it is only a thought. Thoughts are not real. Dissolve the idea that thoughts are real and you will dissolve the suffering.

The investigation of these questions will dissolve the illusion of the bad past experiences. Another way to look at it is to say to yourself, "Just get over it." Do not take it seriously. You will soon be able to say, "Okay that was fun. What's next?" Look at these experiences as they pass through your awareness. Let them come and let them go.

It Feels Like I Do Exist

It feels like I do exist. After you debate this idea for a while, give up the fight and accept that you do exist, just not in the way you used to think. Give into what does exist after rejecting everything that does not. What is left is what is real. Give in to that, because you absolutely do exist as the One and not a separate self.

I Forget Who I Am.

This is a thought, and like all thoughts false. It is not real. Who is having a thought? Why do you identify yourself with all the thoughts that are about you? All thoughts are equally not real, whether they are about you or not.

I Liked My Old Beliefs

I liked the ideas I had about reality, realization and God. I want those back. Are your sure they were not true? You know the answer to this. Change is always scary. Remember when you found out there was no Santa Claus. It was sad at first, but later you acclimated to your new reality.

No matter what you believed or wanted to believe, it is as it is. Get over it and enjoy your life. There is no turning back and it would not matter if you could, because the true reality would not change.

When Your Body Dies

The disciples said to Jesus, "Tell us how our end will come to pass." Jesus said, "Then have you laid bare the beginning, so that you are seeking the end? For the end will be where the beginning is. Blessed is the person who stands at rest in the beginning. And that person will be acquainted with the end and will not taste death.

When your body dies, your mind, body, ego, and identity all dissolves back into the sea of the substrate. What is left is the non-conceptual present moment of self-illuminating presence awareness. The real you continues to be Enlightened and Aware.

If life must not be taken too seriously – then so
neither must death.

Samuel Butler

What You Believe the Afterlife to Be.

What you believe the afterlife to be may be your next illusion. This of course is speculation. In any event, you will still be the pure awareness you are right now. When someone comes in the room and wakes you from sleep by calling your name, you are still aware of their presence even though you are asleep.

I Want to Go To the Next Level

A lot of the so-called and self-proclaimed guru's will maintain the illusion that they are more advanced, better, or different from you. They will string you along and tell you that you have yet to reach the final or advanced level of enlightenment where they are. These so-called gurus are no different from the super heroes in your sleeping dream or on the silver screen. They are fictional characters just like you. They are establishing and reinforcing the concept of separateness that does not exist. It is an illusion and if they do not understand this, they are not enlightened. This is just ego validating itself. WE ARE ALL ONE! The sea of Intelligence energy that makes up the substrate of reality is all there is. There is only the One. There is no separateness outside of the illusion. Prove it to yourself.

Chapter 12

FREQUENTLY ASKED QUESTIONS

Ultimately, you can answer all questions with, "Who is asking?", "Who is doing what and whom is it being done to?" These are universal Advaita answers to most any question concerning reality and illusion. What this means is that if you look to see who is asking you will see that it is no one since the ego is not real, therefore the question is irrelevant. As mentioned earlier, these responses will not be satisfying at first, but after some time you will use these answers to your own questions and it will suffice. Here are some of the more common concepts that many seem to have questions about in the beginning. The answers given here are conceptual and seem more satisfying in the beginning. The purpose of these is to help you solidify your non-conceptual understanding of non-duality reality.

Many questions frequently arise upon finding self-realization. What follows are some of the more common questions. If you do not see the exact question you are looking for, read all of them and you should be able to figure out the answer to your question.

Why is There Bad in the Dream I Am?

Let us suppose that before you went to sleep each night you could create any dream that you wanted. You would create dreams full of pleasure excitement and joy. All would always be exactly as you liked. If you could have an infinite amount of dreams simultaneously in an infinite amount of worlds and universes, experiencing the dream from any point of view you would eventually get bored with a perfect dream. You might want to add a little bit of tension first before you get to the joy. You might want to try dreams that involve suffering, and maybe a lot of suffering. Remember it is only a dream. In fact, with an infinite possibility, you could dream every dream possible. To make things interesting many of these dreams could be quite complex, and filled with surprises. You could get an even greater thrill than you would from a fantastic movie or book where you cannot wait to see what happens next, because you are experiencing it as reality. You would be fully convinced that it was actually happening.

In fact, if the One can have every possible dream one of them will be exactly as the one you are living right now along with all the other infinite number of dreams occurring simultaneously. Your dream is happening exactly like is supposed to go, warts and all. It is just a dream, so watch it happen.

Why do I Feel Lost or Alone After Awakening?

It is a bit shocking to realize that separateness is all a part of an illusion and that in reality there is only the One. At first, it may be disconcerting, but after a while, it becomes liberating as you realize that this very idea of separateness is the cause of all suffering. Give it some time and the truth will set you free.

Should I Share Enlightenment with Others?

As mentioned earlier in the book, this is not for everyone. In order for anyone to recognize their own enlightenment, they must be searching and have a strong desire to find the truth.

For some this may involve the observation of the suffering of others. They may be searching for a solution to problems like global starvation, war, or global warming. For others it may be personal guilt, shame, regret, or self-pity.

The other main motivation that may make one ready to receive this knowledge is the desire to know the truth. These seekers are those who have a burning desire to know what is real. Typically, they have been searching or working for long periods in their life to find perfection in the eyes of God or themselves. This may have involved a great deal of self-discipline, self-denial, and continual striving to earn their place in the spiritual hierarchy. They may have spent significant amount of money through tithing, buying books, taking classes, or working with gurus.

It is not to say that any of the aforementioned attitudes or actions is a prerequisite. The only prerequisites are that they must have a sincere desire to know the truth and a willingness to let go of their preconceived notions once they see the truth. Anyone who desires this knowledge does not have to be worthy or have to have performed a certain amount of hours of self-discipline or extreme training. Everyone is worthy and there is no prerequisite knowledge or training required.

There is no requirement that you have to share this with anyone. In the end, none of these people is real anyway and their awareness is all a part of the overall awareness of the One, just like your own. If you do wish to share this knowledge with those who seem ready then go ahead. If this is what you do and it makes you feel better for having done it, then do it. This all a part of your character's behavior and experience, and it benefits other characters as well, while they live their lives in the illusion.

In order to reduce the undesirable effects in your awareness, you may want to exercise caution when approaching others on the subject. Test the waters a little bit to see if they are searching and are interested. As shocking as it may seem to some reading this book, some people are not searching at all and or either satisfied with where they are on their spiritual journey or are afraid to consider anything else than what they have accepted. That is ok, let them go, they will be fine even if it someone you love.

How do I Know this is not Another Illusion?

If you think back on all the other aspects of the illusion, they all had one thing common. They all required you to have some amount of faith or belief. Strip away everything that may not be true in an illusion and there is nothing left but truth. When you strip away everything that is not true about separateness, there is something left, and that is the Awareness. It is the inescapable conclusion and it never goes away; nothing can alter or harm it in anyway.

Is This Blasphemy?

It depends on how you define blasphemy. What is one faith's belief is another faith's blasphemy. Blasphemy is the defamation of the name of God or gods; or disrespect for something considered sacred. Literally speaking this is not blasphemy because it holds no judgment against anyone or anything else. Awareness does not judge it only observes. The realization that some will come to, may invalidate their previous belief. This in no way invalidates the existence of God, in fact it elevates it from a belief to a non-conceptual knowingness.

Will I Now be Able to do Miracles?

It depends on how you define miracles. Miracles happen every moment all around you and you can choose to be aware of them or not. A never ending series of books could be written about these miracles, but for the moment let us just say that if you start to focus on the Awareness more and subdue the ego you will begin to see and participate in these countless miracles.

The miracles that most people think about are those miracles that happen infrequently, centered around a few unique individuals (not real) and seem to be exceptions to the rules of what we think about as organic reality. These individuals are no more or no less real than you are and they are no more or no less enlightened than you are. Their character's role in this dream is to become Master's of the Illusion." They may or may not be aware of their true selves because their illusion and their ego's have extra layers of illusion to overcome if they believe that their mastery of some part of the illusion makes them enlightened or more enlightened than others. It is not to say that you cannot have both. If the biblical versions and the unfiltered writings of the Gospel of Thomas of the miracles performed by Jesus are correct, then it would seem that Jesus was both a Master of the Illusion and truly enlightened. It would also seem that if you became a Master of the Illusion first it would be extremely difficult to get by your ego to discover your true self.

If creating unusual miracles is what you want to do then go for it, but remember there is only one level of enlightenment and you already have it.

Where do Moses, Jesus, Mohamed, and all the Other Great Religious Leaders Fit into This?

It appears that all were trying to spread the truth in the context of their cultures and their times. It is hard to imagine what the mindset was of a person in a particular culture hundreds or thousands of years ago. Obviously, these great religious figures had a huge impact on the world ever since their arrival. One of the difficult things to do is to try to interpret their messages that religious organizations have filtered through thousands of years of cultural and political change. If you feel you need to continue to have the support of a particular religion then do what makes you feel right.

Is the Ego Just Another Name for the Devil?

Satan or the Devil does not exist. The ego does not exist. Within the illusion, both the ego and Satan are representations of separateness. They are both purported to use deception to convince you that the illusion is real. Your ego is not evil and the Devil, if it even exists within the illusion, is not evil either. The devil is benign and it is playing a role just as your ego is benign and playing a role. There is only the One.

Do I Need to Worship God?

If you want to worship God then worship. If you do not want to worship, then do not. Either way you will not get more enlightened.

Where do I go to Church for This?

You can go to church right where you are every moment of everyday. As far as meeting other likeminded people to ritualize this as a practice, not so much. Most people quickly tire of discussing the awareness amongst those who already understand. It is akin to discussing that the leaves will turn brilliant colors in the fall in North America to someone who has experienced it all their lives. If someone did not have this knowledge because they grew up in sub-Saharan Africa, it would be endless interesting to explain it and answer all their questions about it.

There are blogs available on the internet as well as a virtual meeting place in Second Life on the web. Search for Advaita or non-duality to find these birds of a feather. Most the people you will find here do understand their own enlightenment and may have similar questions as you until they have fully accepted it.

What are Ghosts?

Ghosts are illusions! Are they real within the illusion? I do not know, nor do I care, except to say that really just about anything is possible within the illusion.

Can My True Self be Hurt?

Awareness remains untouched by the content it is observing. If a torrential downpour drenches you as you are walking down the road, only your body and your clothes get wet. The True You remains aloof, untouchable, unaffected. Your true self is immutable by all. It is indestructible and never changing.

Do I Need to Actively be Aware?

Attention and focus are active. Awareness is passive. It requires no effort on your part only the discarding of effort and activity. Awareness is the Observer. You are the Observer. You are Awareness.

Do I Need a Guru?

Many books say it is necessary to work with a guru in order to get it. No one path or unique set of steps is necessary to recognize your enlightenment. If you non-conceptually understand the four primary totalities, you are done. You have reached the highest level. If you have not come to the understanding you may want to look at other points of view from other teachers, if that is what you think you need. There is no unique thing you need to do in order to recognize your enlightenment. The only thing that is important is that you do, if you are interested in receiving the benefits of self-realization during this lifetime. At the end of this lifetime, it will not matter one way or the other if you recognized your enlightenment or not, as you will continue to be aware.

If Life is an Illusion, Why Bother to be Good?

If life is an illusion and nothing matters or is real, why bother to be morally correct or be good. Because your ego will do as it will without free will, it cannot choose to become immoral. If your ego's past experiences do not dictate that it become evil, it will not. Just because you realize your ego is not real and cannot hurt anyone, does not mean that you will become a mass murderer. That would be free will. It is not what your illusion is or does. It would be out of character. If you are reading this book trying to find enlightenment, it is highly unlikely that hurting people intentionally is going to be the action you take because of a deterministic chain of events. Just as sitting on rock indefinitely because you know you are not real is also not possible. If you do not believe it, go sit on a rock for thirty years and let me know how that works out.

Why Continue to Engage in Life?

Why do we continue to work-out, watch our weight, participate in life? Since we now know it is all an illusion, why bother? Why does a flower bloom? Because that is, what it does. Neither the flower nor we have free will. We do what we do. A scorpion will sting because it is a scorpion. Life is being lived. There is more reason after your recognition than before to participate in life. You have removed your shackles and you are free of burdens that once weighted down your life. Sit back and enjoy the show.

Why Do I Still Have So Many Questions?

Questions will eventually fall off. Stick with it. After time, the living reality of non-duality will stabilize and the questions will begin to bore you since they will no longer be relevant.

Should I Start Trying to Live Like a Saint?

Should a self-realized person try to perfect the appearance, become a living Saint? The innate determinism will take over and not allow it. Try to will yourself to hold your breath without ever breathing again. As you begin to breathe again, your ego's innate nature will say, "This is stupid I choose to breath," after the breathing has begun. It will take ownership of the spontaneous actions that occurred beyond its control.

The animated generator of thought is the One. The mind/brain is the receiver and the projector of thought. Try to create a thought. Sit quietly and watch thoughts start to appear. Perfection or saintliness is not a choice. Mother Theresa embodied saintliness all the while having a crisis of faith fearing death as only coldness and non-existence. She too, had no choice.

Is the Ego Bad?

Destruction of the ego is not necessary for the True Self to recognize its own existence. If you desire to get rid of ego, this desire is like any other desire and is an obstacle to achieving enlightenment. Remember desires are part of the ego. Focusing on a desire is focusing on the ego, giving the ego energy and life. The ego is an amazing illusory construct. Marvel in its complexity. Just do not ever believe again the fallacy that it is real.

What about Bad People?

Hitler bears no responsibility, for what happened in WWII. His own illusion was driving his world. Along with everyone else, his actions and thoughts were determined outside his free will. He had no free will. He had to do what he did. He had no choice. In any event, it was just an illusion and not real. He never existed. He was a character actor in a movie. The One dreamt his illusion as it dreams every other illusion.

I know this is hard to accept, because what he did in the illusion was so horrible. He caused so much pain, suffering, death and destruction. Hitler, like your self-identity is not real. There is no separate you and no separate Hitler. No real person felt pain, was killed or anything else. There is only the Immutable One. It cannot be burned by fire, cut by sword, or harmed in any way.

Do I Need to Meditate or Do Something?

You do not need to anything in the strictness sense of the meaning, since you already are perfect, complete Intelligence-Energy. You are already fully aware. Within the appearance of the illusion, we must use the mind and the illusion to prove they do not exist. Meditation can be helpful for some, but is in no way necessary. It may be more helpful in the beginning, until your new understanding settles in, just as much as the illusion has settled in from your early childhood. You can meditate in order to complete the transition from intellectual knowing to non-conceptual knowing. To do this you will need to quiet the mind, focus on your awareness as you meditate and see the mind/body/ego for what it is; an illusion.

Meditating for the purposes of seeking spiritual experiences is not helpful in recognizing your enlightenment. If you want to meditate in order to explore further the illusion, go for it, do not get the two purposes confused. Enjoy the dream.

Enlightenment as conventionally understood does not exist outside of the illusion. The practices of meditation may bring upon some fantastic experiences for some, only after years and years of dedication. It is all meaningless in the context of true enlightenment. These experiences are all make believe and they never really happened. The people having these experiences, like the characters in your dreams, are not real. Neither the characters nor the organic reality ever existed. When you wake up you see them as the illusion they really are.

Chapter 13

CONCLUSIONS

You are now awake. You have attained lucid wakefulness. You are the Dreamer. You are God. You are the One. Your purpose in life is to experience and enjoy the ride.

I did not write this book. I witnessed the thoughts bubbling up and watched my illusory self write it. This book and its author are all an illusion. My illusory self had no choice, because this is what it does and I watched it happen. You wrote this book as much as I. Your search is over.

Remember the Zen saying, before enlightenment chop wood, carry water, after enlightenment, chop wood carry water. Get on with the chopping and carrying. Now that you are free, enjoy life to its fullest.

For more information about Awaken to the Here and Now, visit the website. www.awakentothehereandnow.com.

Made in the USA